I0068020

Women Who Rise

Women Who Rise

Ambition, Motherhood, and the Right to Want More

Rocio Ariela Izquierdo

BEP
BUSINESS EXPERT PRESS
Leader in applied, concise business books

Women Who Rise: Ambition, Motherhood, and the Right to Want More

Copyright © Business Expert Press, LLC, 2026.

Cover design by Soledad Ldu0ueña

Interior design by S4Carlisle Publishing Services, Chennai, India

All rights reserved. No part of this publication may be reproduced, stored in a retrieval system, or transmitted in any form or by any means—electronic, mechanical, photocopy, recording, or any other except for brief quotations, not to exceed 400 words, without the prior permission of the publisher.

First published in 2025 by
Business Expert Press, LLC
222 East 46th Street, New York, NY 10017
www.businessexpertpress.com

ISBN-13: 978-1-63742-914-3 (paperback)
ISBN-13: 978-1-63742-915-0 (e-book)

Human Resource Management and Organizational Behavior Collection

First edition: 2025

10 9 8 7 6 5 4 3 2 1

EU SAFETY REPRESENTATIVE
Mare Nostrum Group B.V.
Mauritskade 21D
1091 GC Amsterdam
The Netherlands
gpsr@mare-nostrum.co.uk

Dedication

To the CEOs who trusted me with their stories and were an inspiration to my investigation. Thank you for teaching me what a leader is.

To my mum who always trusted me and encouraged me to be myself and study Political Science. Thank you for being there.

To Gonzalo, my partner in this life, who always loves me and believes in me. Thank you for being my rock.

For people who never give up and dare to dream big.

Description

Through over a decade of working in business organizations that support managerial growth and collaborating directly with CEOs of national and multinational companies, I encounter leaders who inspired me with a simple yet powerful message:

"Women don't have to choose between having a family, working, and being successful."

"Women Who Rise: Ambition, Motherhood, and the Right to Want More," explores the real, unfiltered, and intimate experiences of women who have reached the highest levels of leadership—all while balancing family responsibilities.

Based on my master's thesis research, this book dives into their decision-making processes, leadership styles, and the challenges they faced while navigating both personal and professional demands. Unlike traditional leadership books, through compelling case studies and practical advice, this book provides an essential guide for young professionals pursuing managerial careers, business leaders, and readers interested in management, and public policy.

By learning from those who have walked this path, readers will gain actionable insights into navigating the conflicting demands of career and care. It is my hope that this book becomes a go-to manual for women with difficult choices ahead of them, whether they are in business school or already stepping into leadership roles.

Contents

List of Figures xi
Preface xiii

Chapter 1   Why Are We Talking About Care? 1
Chapter 2   How to Build Your Managerial Career and
             Earn Your Place? 17
Chapter 3   From CEO to Chief Executive Mom Officer 51
Chapter 4   What's Next? 101

Bibliography 105
About the Author 113
Index 115

List of Figures

Figure 1   Activity Rates by Sex and Income Quintile (2017) 7

Figure 2   Female Employment Rates by Income Quintile 7

Figure 3   Participation and Hours in Unpaid Domestic
            Work by Sex...9

Figure 4   Unpaid Domestic Work vs. Paid Work Hours
            by Sex (2013) 9

Figure 5   Women in Leadership Positions in the Business
            Sector...12

Figure 6   CEO Gender Distribution by Company 13

Figure 7   Female Managers' Experience with Discrimination 38

Figure 8   Comparison of Male and Female Management
            Styles...57

Figure 9   Family Rituals 89

Preface

One of the unique features that the 20th century witnessed was the reconfiguration of the middle class and the labor market transformations. Alongside the increased access to education, the capitalist relations and labor relations in large companies reconverted due to the economic opening, foreign capital mobility, and the privatization of many different companies. Together with the evolution and professionalization of large companies, such reconversion allowed for the development of a techno-bureaucratic ruling elite known as "*managers.*"

Managers are responsible for achieving management goals as well as for the innovation of companies, thus combining corporate policy compliance with resource organization, planning, control, and direction to meet the objectives of such corporate policy and management plan.

Companies typically feature more men in leading positions. In Argentina and worldwide, few women can be found in strategic leadership positions. The distribution of jobs at the bottom of the pyramid of companies is more equitable between men and women, but, in higher ranks, men are the ones generally in charge of resource management and decision making. This is particularly evident when analyzing the composition of the boards of prominent business organizations and bi-national chambers of commerce. In Argentina, the percentage of women present ranges between only 3 and 7 percent according to studies from IDEA in 2018 and the Latin American Justice and Gender Team (ELA) of 2021.

These numbers have been bringing many discussions in labor policy and the public agenda as regards the role of women in the labor market, the challenges faced for being responsible for child and elder care, as well as the time allocated to remunerative and nonremunerative tasks. Caregiving and all tasks involving the development and well-being of people comprise elements typical of paid jobs together with emotional elements and a network of complex relationships.

Women often face difficult choices when it comes to balancing their careers and family responsibilities. The burden of care work, which includes both caring for children and elderly family members as well as self-care, falls disproportionately on women. This can make it difficult for women to pursue career opportunities, especially those that require a significant time commitment or are not flexible enough to accommodate caregiving responsibilities.

The unequal distribution of care work between men and women also contributes to gender inequality in the workplace. Women are often forced to take on lower-paying and less stable jobs that offer more flexibility to accommodate caregiving responsibilities. This can lead to a "motherhood penalty" in which women who have children are penalized in the workplace, earning lower salaries and having fewer opportunities for career advancement.

Addressing the unequal distribution of care work is essential for achieving gender equality in the workplace. This can include policies such as paid parental leave, affordable childcare, and flexible work arrangements that allow both men and women to balance their work and caregiving responsibilities. By reducing the burden of care work on women, we can create an equal and just society.

However, this inequality is an analytical dimension affecting not only women from the lowest social quintiles but also female managers. Women from the lowest social quintiles find it extremely difficult to access the formal labor market and eventually have to opt for the informal labor market and poorly paid jobs. Although less studied, the universe of female managers is also filled with specific inequalities about the possibility of growing in their management careers and accessing decision-making positions and boards of directors. More is known about inequalities in low-income social sectors, but there are few studies about women at the top of the organizational pyramid in Argentina. Social sciences in this country, unlike in the international field, still need to study this social actor in greater depth as it is a key aspect of the labor transformations currently taking place.

The aforementioned inequality is present in two large dimensions:

1. Families and their organizations
2. Management careers and their construction

Family organization dynamics were transformed due to the evolution of labor market dynamics and the need for both family members to work in order to achieve the family's full enhancement. Nevertheless, women are still solely responsible for family care tasks in matters related to food, presence at events, and affective development, among others.

Women in leadership positions face many problems derived from having to fulfill multiple roles; they are caregivers in the family sphere and business leaders in the social-labor sphere. Therefore, they have to find solutions when developing their management careers.

This book is the result of my MA thesis where I analyzed the tests, the difficulties, and the challenges that a group of female managers had to face in their management career path. These women currently occupy the highest leadership positions in private companies and business organizations in Argentina.

I have worked for eight years in business organizations dedicated to the training, relationship, and growth of managers in Argentina. I have worked for four years directly with CEOs of national and multinational companies on different topics that allow for the building of relations with actors in politics, trade unionism, and civil society, including social inclusion and diversity issues. During this time, the different profiles of women leaders who I met and worked with, along with their vision of leadership and their unique decision-making methods, awakened an intellectual interest in me. As a consequence, I started to consider studying female managers and the multidimensionality and transversality of inequality within the social field of female managers, which has been little researched so far.

While conducting my research I wondered what difficulties related to family planning did, these women undergo during their management careers. How did they reconcile working life development with family life development? What labor and personal costs did they have to bear?

The starting point hereof is the assumption that higher socioeconomic sectors develop specific forms of time management as well as more commodified support networks with the aim of having more time to develop their management careers.

I interviewed 11 women and 3 men CEOs, directors, and business leaders from March to September 2020. When carrying out the interviews, the ASPO (Preventive and Mandatory Social Isolation) was in force in the Argentine territory. This situation affected the way to conduct the interviews, and, hence, these had to take place through Zoom and Skype videoconferencing platforms; these people were interviewed while at their homes during working hours, post-working hours, and/or days of leave.

Fragments of the conversations are quoted to show the development of the central points of study hereof and to provide examples that support the statements made and reaffirm the concepts included in this book. To maintain confidentiality and safeguard the anonymity of the interviewees and the companies that they refer to, I have changed all of their names. During the interviews, verbal language was not the only aspect taken into account; the executives' nonverbal language was also noted and considered.

Since trust relations had already been built, I was able to successfully carry out the interviews and obtain relevant information. Having worked in business organizations directly with women and men CEOs in multidimensional projects for a term of nine years allowed me to build trust and close relations with them. These relationships made it easier for me to ensure their participation make them feel motivated about the topic and interview them directly between March and July 2020.

The women interviewed for this research have the following characteristics:

- Their ages range between 33 and 50 years old.
- They all consider their mothers, fathers, and family in general as "*middle-class workers*" (one or both parents working in the formal labor market).
- Considering the 11 women leaders interviewed:
  - 20 percent obtained a degree in social sciences such as political science
  - 20 percent pursued technical careers such as actuary or statistics
  - 60 percent got a business degree including business administration and accounting

- As regards the universities attended, 55 percent studied at public universities—mainly UBA (University of Buenos Aires)—while 27 percent studied at private universities.
- Out of the 11 women interviewed, 7 of them obtained postgraduate diplomas.
- Eight of the female executives interviewed started to work while still attending their undergraduate studies, and three of them did so after obtaining their university degrees.
- Nine of the women interviewed are in a relationship, seven are married, and two are divorced.
- Eight women have children of their own. One of the interviewees has stepchildren from her spouse's previous relationship, and two of them have no sons or daughters.

This book is divided into four chapters. The first chapter explores the question of why care matters when discussing women's work and opportunities. It examines the dimensions of care and division of labor, showing how societal expectations around caregiving shape women's career choices, access to opportunities, and realities. Through the lens of building both a paid and care work schedules, this chapter highlights the invisible labor women often carry and how those expectations reinforce the glass ceiling, with subtle but yet persistent limits of advancement, and the concrete ceiling, a more rigid and self-perpetuating barrier.

The second chapter examines how women built their managerial careers and the people and values that influenced this journey. It traces the early impact on family values and expectations, then follows the first steps into the managerial path and the rise of formal management development. This chapter also sheds light on what often remains hidden within managerial careers—subtle gender stereotypes, unspoken rules, and patterns of discrimination. By making this dynamics visible, it highlights strategies needed to overcome these challenges and barriers and earn a lasting place in leadership.

The third chapter confronts the reality of being both a leader and a mother, showing how women refuse to accept they must choose between career, family, and success. It takes on the difficulties of returning to work after maternity leave, the role of supportive partners, and the social pressures placed on women who do not have children, This chapter explores the Female Manager's Manual—an unwritten guide distilled from the experiences of the women interviewed—which offers practical examples of how navigate leadership and family responsibilities. Alongside it, there is a checklist that serves as tips and strategies passed on to future leaders.

Finally, the last chapter looks ahead, asking what comes next by reflecting on the ongoing challenges society must address to create environments where leaders can truly thrive and have it all. More than a closing note, it is a call to action—inviting readers, leaders, scholars, and policymakers to keep this topic on the public agenda, to continue researching female manager's development, and to work collectively toward a more inclusive future in business and management.

CHAPTER 1

Why Are We Talking About Care?

Nowadays, it is quite often to hear on the news, social media, and even companies and state policies the importance of care. The action of care has been transformed and deconstructed from the last century and especially in the last years. In the past, it was invisible, something that as a society we did not think about. However, we can see debates addressing the topic but not always in a rightful way.

When we first talked about care, it was considered an activity belonging to the private business of women. It was the activity and set of responsibilities that nourish them, the symbolic elements that allow women to live a full life in society. The main thing that defined them. Now, the concept of care is part of the public agenda of the nation-states.

Care is understood as the set of activities that are necessary to satisfy minimum needs in order to support the existence and reproduction of people. This involves directly providing care and attention to dependent people—such as children and adolescents—as well as older, sick or disabled people (Pautassi and Zibecchi 2013)

Since the 1970s and 1980s, feminists started questioning the traditional gender roles of men and women within families, society, and public life. Considering the concept of the sexual division of labor as a social organization based on gender-exclusive dichotomies, it becomes clear that the public and private spheres of life are part of a social formation. In each of these spheres, men and women, respectively, are assigned a specific type of work. The sexual division of labor is part of social relations that articulates production and reproduction.

Traditional gender roles have historically assigned women the primary responsibility for caregiving tasks, including raising children and taking care of the elderly and other dependent family members. This has contributed to the unequal distribution of care responsibilities between men and women, which in turn has limited women's opportunities for professional development and advancement.

The normalization of women's ability to take care of others is a product of deeply ingrained cultural and societal expectations around gender roles. These expectations reinforce the idea that women are naturally suited to caregiving tasks, while men are expected to be providers and breadwinners. This gendered division of labor has perpetuated gender inequality in the workplace and beyond.

It is important to recognize that caregiving tasks are not solely the responsibility of women. Men, too, have a role to play in caring for their families and dependent family members. By challenging traditional gender roles and promoting greater equality in the distribution of caregiving responsibilities, we can create a more just and equitable society. This can involve policies that support both men and women in balancing their work and caregiving responsibilities, such as paid parental leave, flexible work arrangements, and affordable childcare.

The historical sexual division of labor presented men as actors inherent in public life and characterized them as strong providers. Women, on the other hand, were viewed as actors inherent in private life and were associated with domestic and care tasks; their function was only to sustain human life, and they did not take any roles in the paid labor market (Carrasco 2001).

Considering economic concepts and definitions, unpaid work—housework being the most typical form thereof—shares some characteristics with certain forms of paid work: the use of time and energy or the opportunity cost for a specific purpose. This is the reason why housework should not actually be considered a leisure or discretionary activity but, instead, a part of the division of labor. It is an activity for the production of goods and services within the home, unlike work activities that are aimed at earning money in order to purchase consumer goods.

Later on, the multidimensionality of care was studied in more detail from the point of view of social policy.[1] The term "*care*," hence, refers to self-care and the direct and interpersonal care of others. It also extends to domestic and household tasks, the management of care responsibilities, schedule coordination, interactions with social institutions, and the supervision of caregiving activities. In this sense and taking into account the point of view of psychological care, care means being aware of the dependency of others since it implies carrying out physical actions that can be measured chronologically as well as actions that involve responsibility, affection, and care.

On the other hand, caring for older people[2] relates to the well-being and quality of life of those who cannot fend for themselves as regards their everyday tasks. The degree of care required is closely related to the level of dependency of the older adult, and the lack or loss of physical, mental,

---

[1]Valeria Esquivel (2011) states that care refers to an interpersonal relationship regardless of its remuneration or the place where such care task is carried out:

> *The care economy shifts the focus from the costs of those who provide care—women—to the contributions to the wellbeing of those who receive such care.* (Esquivel 2011, 10)

This logic allows for the visibility of care tasks performed at home as well as the differences in genders and social classes.

Laura Pautassi (2013) states that women who dedicate time to care activities, including self-care activities, see their work trajectories affected by the time distribution necessary to carry out all these activities. In turn, this affects their salaries and gives birth to a discriminatory situation as regards their male peers.

Corina Rodríguez Enríquez (2014) claims that the importance of care has increased in the public agenda due to the visibility of the economic dynamics of care, the understanding of the value of care and its social organization, and the importance of public policies to organize care activities in a more equitable way.

María Ángeles Durán (2016) suggests measuring care not only through physical actions but also through considering the degree of dedication, responsibility, and time availability. She states that care tasks are carried out by individuals who care for themselves as well as unpaid care networks—especially families—and paid care workers.

[2]María Ángeles Durán (2016) claims that old age and illness are often associated due to the loss of vigor, the possibility to suffer physical disabilities, the deterioration of cognitive abilities, and the illnesses present in both. As the passage of time is inevitable, most developed economies have social security and protection systems to allow older people's access to resources that guarantee their subsistence.

or sensory autonomy is pondered. In most societies, these care tasks are solely carried out by women, regardless of their work and social activities. This type of work is invisible in societies and is associated with classic stereotypes about women.

As a result, women's disproportionate responsibility for caregiving and domestic work can limit their opportunities for professional development and advancement. This is because the demands of care work often require women to work longer hours, leaving them with less time and energy to devote to their careers.

Moreover, traditional gender stereotypes have long associated women with caregiving qualities, such as empathy and communicativeness, which are often seen as incompatible with leadership roles in the public sphere. This can create a *"double bind"* for women who are expected to be both caring and nurturing in their personal lives, while also being ambitious and assertive in their professional lives.

Building the Paid and Care Work Schedule

The social, economic, and political factors that have contributed to the increase in women´s participation in labor markets have indeed been accompanied by criticism of traditional gender roles and the dominant social order that has perpetuated gender inequality.

At the heart of this critique is the recognition that every social organization has a dominant group that defines, imposes, and universalizes its values and vision of culture and world organization. This, in turn, reflects on social relations and structures, the forms of relating to others, power relations, and the knowledge and understanding of the world, and even customs and the uses of language. In this process, men and women have actively appropriated these social structures throughout history, transforming them into typified behavior.

The increase in women's participation in labor markets did not only deeply transform the role of women and gave a new meaning to the family as an institution but also caused a great economic and social impact on the world. The Organization for Economic Co-operation and Development (OECD) claims that women's participation in the labor market helps and influences the development of economies by increasing the economy's GDP as well as the GDP per capita. The OECD, like other international organizations, state that, in order for economies to be sustainable in the long term and contribute to poverty reduction, the resources available must be used most efficiently and, thus, the incorporation of women in paid jobs becomes necessary.

Equality is a central issue on the Economic Commission for Latin America and the Caribbean's (ECLAC) agenda, with a focus on Latin American countries achieving the Sustainable Development Goals set by the UN regarding the building of inclusive societies by ending poverty and inequality within sustainable environments. Labor equity, understood as the access of men and women to equal opportunities to take part in the labor market, represents a significant dimension of gender equity in all societies working toward equality.

In the case of Latin America, the International Labor Organization (ILO) reviews the studies carried out by the economic consultants McKinsey and PWC in the 2017 report "Women in Business Management: Gaining Momentum in Latin America and the Caribbean." These studies show that, if women's participation in the economy increases, then the annual GDP of Latin America would rise 34 percent and that, if the gender gap in the labor market in Argentina and Brazil is closed, the local GDPs would increase between 12 and 19 percent year-on-year. Following studies drafted by the World Bank, ILO, and ECLAC, the number of women participating in the labor market has been increasing since the 1960s, thus affecting the lives of millions of women in the region as well as the forms of daily life and family organization.

According to the statistics by the Labor Overview Report for Latin America and the Caribbean 2017 drafted by ILO, approximately 117 million women in Latin America and the Caribbean take part in the labor force. This number represents a women participation rate of 50.2 percent, an unprecedented figure in the region's labor markets, given that such percentage had never been higher than 45 percent.

However, and at the same time, this does not mean that the existing gender gaps are closed. The percentage of men's participation in the labor market is of 74.4 percent, that is, 24.2 percent higher than the women labor force participation rate. In addition, ECLAC concluded that the COVID-19 health crisis deepens these differences and evidenced the unfair socioeconomic organization of care in Latin America.

Women in privileged socioeconomic positions have more resources available to access the current labor market and pursue careers that allow for the acquisition of care goods. Households with higher incomes are those in which two or more family members have paid jobs. Individuals' needs are classified into those satisfied by the market and those specific to the private sector without regard to the classical model of paid work/consumption. Therefore, there is a need for public policies that support the efforts made by families and individuals toward their development since families and households are not the same.

The National State recognizes families as units that protect property, provide care, ensure the well-being of their individual members, and inherently involve love and intimacy as the space opposite to the rules and regulations of political organizations and modern economy. The development of social relations and interactions within families as well as the use and management of resources, such as the emotional aspect of relationships and bonds, may be different from our preexisting conceptions and ideas about families.

Within family units, the division of labor is based on the economic activities that generate income and the domestic work activities that generate use values. Likewise, family units acquire behaviors and beliefs directly related to the social class to which they belong, in search of the material reproduction of the biological and social conditions of such group.

The whole society aspires to be part of those households with access to more significant goods, "even if, in practice, this means adopting a lifestyle in which activities related to care and self-realization are suppressed by other demands on time (work and consumption demands)." (Himmelweit 2005, 266–267)

The statistical dossier commemorating the 110th International Women's Day (2021) drafted by the Argentine Institute of Statistics and Census (INDEC)[3] showed that women with higher educational levels come from and, in turn, form households of medium or high socioeconomic

---

[3]This dossier compares the employment activity and unemployment rate of women of different economic quintiles.

status. They can even triple their levels of employment and employability in comparison to women with less formal education. This implies having more resources to support their participation in the labor market by resorting to children and elder care private services (Figures 1 and 2).

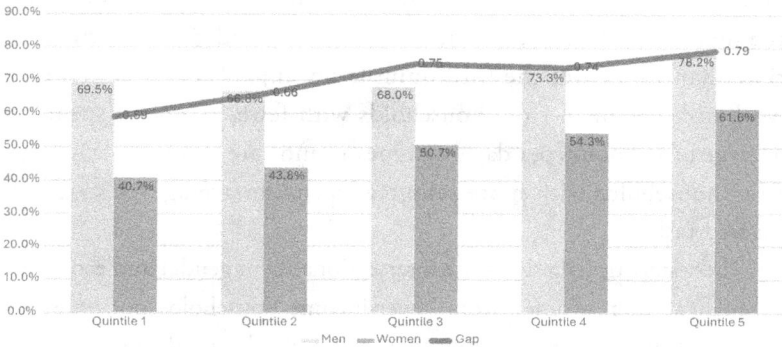

Figure 1 Activity Rates by Sex and Income Quintile (2017)

Total of surveyed agglomerates.

Third quarter of 2017.

Source: DGEMyEL–MTEySS, Based on EPH–INDEC information.

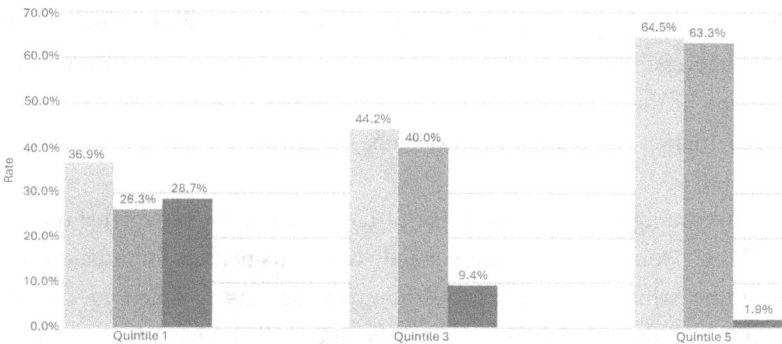

Figure 2 Female Employment Rates by Income Quintile

Total: 31 Urban agglomerates. Third quarter of 2020.

In women with less income, the unemployment rate is **15 times higher** than that of those who belong to the highest quintile.

Source: Based on EPH–INDEC information.

As regards paid work, the gender gap in households with fewer resources is more pronounced than in households of the last quintile, where, on average, women and men spend a similar amount of time working in the labor market. However, in both the first and the fifth quintile, the gender gap is present when considering the time spent on unpaid work tasks, although it is more noticeable in the first quintile than in the fifth. Lower-income women spend significantly more time than women of the fifth quintile on unpaid care and domestic work tasks. Women from households with fewer resources spend an average of 7.2 hours per day on domestic and care tasks, while women from households with more resources spend an average of 3.7 hours on said tasks.

These statistics highlight the intersectionality of gender and economic inequality, where women from lower-income households not only face challenges in accessing the labor market but also bear a disproportionate burden of unpaid care and domestic work. This further limits their opportunities for professional and personal development, perpetuating the cycle of economic inequality.

The survey further claims that this social gap is caused by a combination of factors. These factors include the higher amount of care tasks for dependent people, the difficulty of delegating care tasks to extra-domestic spaces due to the public sector's insufficient offer, and the inaccessibility to hire such services in a private manner. Given that, women of the last quintile have access to the worst opportunities in the labor market, as well as the existence of gender stereotypes regarding care tasks.

According to the results of the 2013 Time Use Survey carried out by INDEC, women spend approximately 6.4 hours per day on unpaid tasks at home, while men dedicate 3.4 hours to such tasks. When we analyze activities linked to paid work, the difference is little since the men labor force participation rate is higher than their female counterparts. Women's participation rate, on the other hand, is greater in respect to unpaid domestic and care tasks (Figure 3).

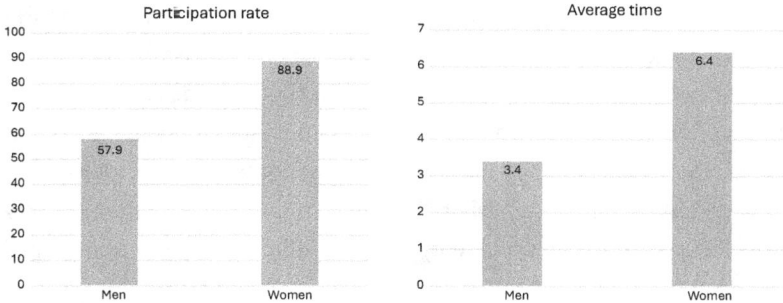

Figure 3 Participation and Hours in Unpaid Domestic Work by Sex

The population considered is aged 18 and over. Total: National and urban. Third quarter of 2013.

Source: DGEMyEL–MTEySS, Based on information from the Survey on Unpaid Work and Time Use by INDEC.

The results of the Time Use Survey in the City of Buenos Aires are similar to those of the Argentine Survey of Time Use of 2013 carried out by INDEC. Women dedicate approximately 1 hour per day less than men do to paid tasks in the labor market, but they spend 3.27 hours on domestic tasks while men spend only 1.57 hours on such tasks. When analyzing care tasks, women dedicate 5.27 hours per day to these tasks while men spend 3.42 hours on them (INDEC 2013). The organization of care relates to the behavior regarding care of families, the State and the market institutions, as well as social and community organizations (Figure 4).

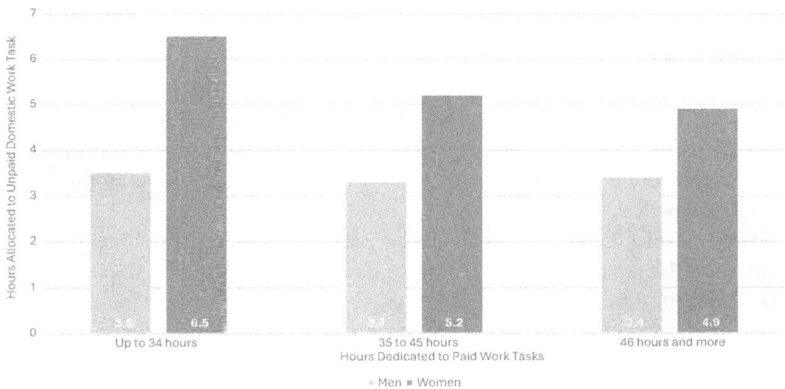

Figure 4 Unpaid Domestic Work vs. Paid Work Hours by Sex (2013)

Source: INDEC. Survey on Unpaid Work and Time Use (2013).

In this sense, the pursuit of professional careers by women from households with access to specific resources is influenced, in part, by the dedication of men to care and parenting tasks. As a result, women are not forced to abandon their professional career development for family development.

In the Argentine law, male and female workers' care responsibility and co-responsibility are generally limited to maternity and paternity leave issues that explicitly stereotype gender roles. The concept of "equal opportunities" entails discrimination regarding gender inequality and socioeconomic structural inequalities. Labor regulation on maternity and paternity leaves does not currently recognize care as universal children's right or distinguish the particularities of the labor market. Therefore, this becomes a right exclusive to people in the formal labor market.

At the same time, regulations do not recognize men's responsibilities[4] regarding the development and comprehensive care of children; Argentine paternity leaves grant fathers only two business days off work. Therefore, it is clear that rules governing family care entail a double inequality: socioeconomic and gender inequality.

Glass and Concrete Ceilings

In Argentina, as in the region and the rest of the world, few women occupy strategic command positions as Managers or CEOs.[5]

At the base of the pyramid of companies, the distribution of jobs is more equitable between men and women, but, when moving

---

[4]Pautassi and Rico (2011) recognize that it is urgent and necessary to consider care issues from a transversal point of view. The National State must extend paid leaves for fathers to complement maternity leaves and give rise to new paid leaves for mothers and fathers, including during parenting stages other than the early-childhood period.

[5]The term CEO (Chief Executive Officer) refers to the position held by the highest responsible authority in a company, under either that name or that of Executive President, Director, or General Manager.

The concept of CEO has a social element since it represents a social elite with economic and political power. Authors such as Wright Mills include top managers within what they call "*power elites*" (1956), which are made up of individuals occupying key command positions in leading organizations of society—in a military and in an economic and political sense (Luci and Szlechter 2014).

The title may vary, but it is clear that the main function of CEOs is to administrate and manage private or public profit or nonprofit entities.

up in rank, mostly men occupy management and decision-making positions.[6]

This aspect contradicts the vision and organizational discourse that considers management careers as neutral in terms of gender and only related to each individual's capacity.[7] This network is a global social phenomenon with horizontal segmentation (women tend to be more present in specific labor market segments) and vertical segmentation (women tend to occupy positions of relatively lower power).

Management careers are sexually regulated by an informal and imperceptible *"glass ceiling"* that reinforces the elusive nature of the sexual dimension present in this career since, in theory, everyone has an equal chance to succeed (Luci 2016). Although women achieve higher academic goals than men, success in management careers is limited by both external and internal factors—glass and concrete ceiling, respectively. As a result, highly qualified women decide to reject job promotions, modify their working hours, and look for positions that allow some flexibility to reconcile professional tasks with care tasks (Figure 5).

---

[6]CEOs carry out companies' internal and external functions related to the development of company strategies and the supervision of corporate processes, as well as the report of various issues, goals, achievements, and problems to external actors, shareholders, and investors. The qualities and characteristics needed for such position refer to the capacity and ability to make decisions. These decisions are related to:

- The company's strategies and values
- Planning and setting goals, objectives, and action plans for the short, medium, and long term in order to achieve the company's general objectives
- Adapting to micro- and macro-economic challenges in search of those objectives
- Representing and being an example of those values as well as motivating team members to work collaboratively in pursuit of the company's goals
- Maintaining an open dialogue with both internal and external actors
- Organizing and managing available resources
- Controlling and verifying that the action plan is executed effectively according to the goals set

[7]Holding a management or executive position in a company requires not only to perform well as regards labor functions in the strict sense but also certain personality traits. These are typified and assessed by companies and include traits such as confidence and self-confidence, autonomy, emotional stability, flexibility, and ability to adapt to changes and uncertainties, proactivity, as well as self-motivation and ability to deal with frustration, pressure, and problems. Both the capacity to reach the leadership position and the capacity to keep it are equally important, since the environment is very competitive and changes rapidly.

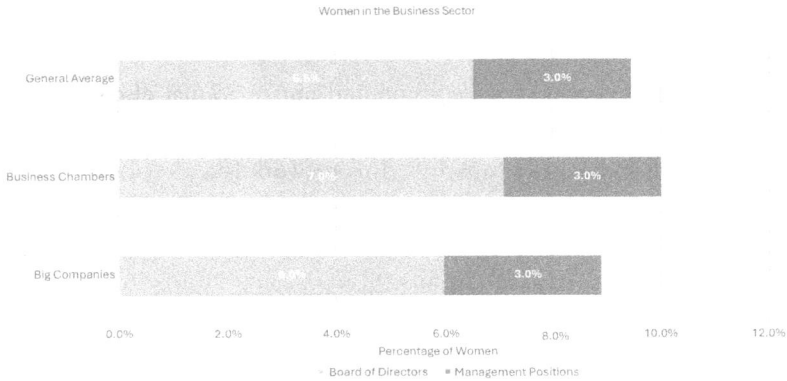

Figure 5 Women in Leadership Positions in the Business Sector

Source: Report sex and power. Who rules in Argentina?

Regarding internal barriers—concrete ceiling—the Operational Director of Facebook in the United States, Sheryl Sanberg (2013), sets out a new concept: Even though women can overcome institutional barriers to access management positions, there are internal barriers that lead women to feel the need to take on greater responsibilities and to feel more pressure when making decisions.

> *It is not about working to break down any of these barriers— internal/external—but fighting on two fronts: cultural conceptions of women in leadership roles as well as the guarantee that public and private institutions are working to meet women's demands regarding the necessary conditions to occupy these leadership positions.* (Sandberg 2013, 9)

There are cases of women in leadership positions who must *"pay the price"*—either because of an own conscious decision or because of the constructs and decisions that they face throughout their management careers—of not having a partner and/or children and be stigmatized in their executive roles. It is generally considered that women who pursue management and leadership careers neglect their families and their children's comprehensive development. Likewise, and as discussed in the following chapters, deciding to start a family is a turning point and a choice that affects the entire management career. Having children affects the desire of professional fulfillment and promotion because time begins to be divided between the professional career and leadership responsibilities and family life.

In this sense, *"discretionary time"*—time apart from paid work activities, unpaid care work tasks, and self-care activities—questions the definition of individuals' well-being and measures temporal autonomy. Following this line of analysis, while free time concerns the time allocated to the three aforementioned activities, discretionary time refers to the time that a person actually needs to spend on such activities (Figure 6).

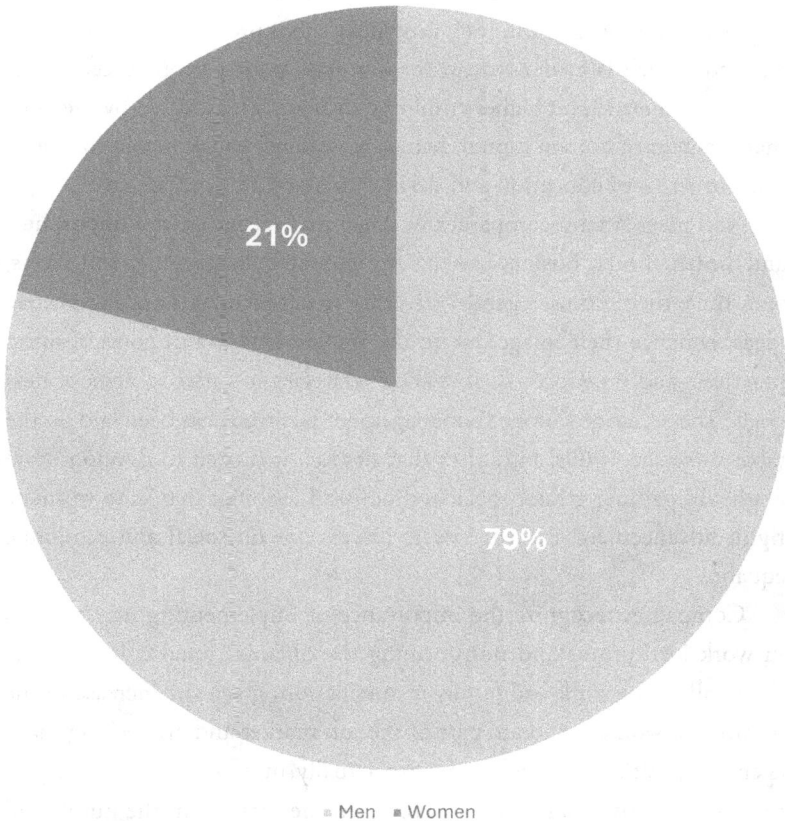

■ Men   ■ Women

Figure 6 CEO Gender Distribution by Company

Source: ACTEMP ILO Business Survey (2017).

The professional success of women in management careers depends largely on family organization and the division of domestic and care tasks. The current management career model is based on an asymmetrical division of domestic work. Even today, women are the breadwinners and the ones who manage family's interests in search of its comprehensive development, mostly excluding men from domestic concerns and tasks.

Following the study by Florencia Luci on managers' development in Argentina, managers, directors, and CEOs work an average of 10.5 hours per day. They rarely leave the office before 7:30 p.m. or 8:00 p.m., which can give rise to family tensions and affect both work performance and family development. These asymmetries in the organization of families make it difficult for women to fully pursue their professional careers as they are constantly trying to reconcile work responsibilities with family responsibilities. As a result, their individual labor productivity is adversely affected, which is evidenced by, for example, poor performance, higher absenteeism rates, and higher employee turnover rates caused by the poor management of human capital, female workforce, and women's contributions in terms of education and decision making to work schemes.

Nowadays, many companies in Argentina recognize the importance and the benefits for businesses of having women in management positions, and, thus, they promote gender diversity to access talents and innovative ideas, enhance their image due to the implementation of good business practices, and transform their market strategies in order to achieve new goals. The access of women to management positions has been laid on the table since the 1960s, but, after that decade, it started to develop more gradually, gaining greater social and political visibility thanks to women's rights advancement and the rise of discussions on social and economic equality.

Companies recognize the importance of implementing new policies in work institutions and transforming the organizational culture in order to allow for work and family reconciliation, given the increase in the number of women who are part of the job market and are seeking management positions. Mixed teams are actually more effective in decision making and crisis management. However, the increase in the number of women occupying management positions did not weaken the gender stereotype formation as regards social behaviors, decision-making processes, and leadership capacities. Women are criticized for behaviors associated with both women and men.

As analyzed in the following chapters, women have to build leadership by confronting constructs of peers, both women and especially men. In part, these constructs presuppose that there are behaviors more associated with *male leadership*—men are regarded as decisive leaders and strong decision makers, but women with these characteristics are seen as cold and emotionally distant—and *female leadership*—women are considered to have a greater connection with team members, but, many times, this fails to make them be seen as authoritarian, ambitious, or even competent in the pursuit of company objectives.

Most men are able to pursue their careers and professional success since women work at home or work part-time and decide to put an end to their own professional development, thus allowing men to disregard domestic life tasks and concerns. Executive women, on the other hand, must personally take charge of building a domestic network that supports family in order to continue developing their management careers. By carrying out paid work tasks—and developing their management careers—women have been earning enough money to delegate the tasks that they personally carried out at their homes (Himmelweit 2005). This corresponds to the culture of *"time macho":* a relentless competition to work harder, stay longer, work at night, travel the world, and bill additional hours in order to have an international career, which is often the case of many professionals (Slaughter 2012).

Studies show that women occupying management positions are married to men working in activities that allow them more independency and, likewise, support their wives' professional pursuit.

Due to their gender, female executives must strengthen their commitment and involvement because they are assumed to be in charge of childcare and household tasks, thus allegedly finding it more difficult to maintain a high level of energy during long working days. (Luci 2016, 56)

In addition to this strong support from male spouses, female executives have also family and commodified domestic care networks that help with childcare tasks. Companies can, together with public policies, help promote a culture where decisions to marry and have children do not imply abandoning the professional career. Given the changes observed in men's behaviors as regards child-rearing, the question is whether companies will look for the opportunity to meet their staff's new expectations and needs. Will companies, in order to continue developing and achieve success, contribute to employees' search of balance between paid work tasks and family care responsibilities and foster change in public labor policies?

CHAPTER 2

How to Build Your Managerial Career and Earn Your Place?

Management careers involve specific rules, social behaviors, stages, and moments. The social practices that coordinate the relations between managers occupying top management positions are directly related to company's values and career plans. Managers' values and career trajectories, in addition to their professional skills and experience, also play a role as regards their access to management positions and companies' boards. I identify four stages of women's management careers:

- The role and influence of family values
- The way in which these values impacted their decision to pursue a professional career
- The challenges, difficulties, and critical decisions involved in their management careers as well as the role of mentors
- The sometimes visible, but often normalized, discriminatory situations faced

Families and Values Shaping the Beginning

The development of women leaders' corporate careers begins as soon as they graduate from high school. Most of these leaders described the members of their nuclear families as workers of immigrant European origin who considered that attending university and growing professionally within big companies were the ways to comply with the intergenerational self-improvement goal. The characteristics and conceptions of these women's family core are not usually different from those mentioned by men. Both regard their families as *very standard middle-class families from Argentina*,"[8] in which one or, in some cases, both parents had paid jobs.

In addition, most women in these families worked at home carrying out household chores and care tasks, and children mainly attended public universities. The results of Jorge Jorrat's 2008 study show that, in Argentina, people usually identify themselves as middle class rather than working class, given their professions.

> *People with all levels of education and from all household income quintiles identify themselves as middle class, while the opposite is true in the case of lower and working classes. There are more people from lower objective categories who identify themselves as middle class than people from higher categories who identify themselves as low or working class.* (Jorrat 2008, 14)

The main purpose of these families was to make it easier for their children to obtain a university degree and pursue a professional career. Hence, they did not pressure their children to start working at an early age, although many of them decided to do so in order to access the corporate world and start developing their professional careers. One of the male executives interviewed perfectly summarized the characteristics and the origins of these families.

---

[8]Following the work of Jorge Raúl Jorrat (2008) on popular perceptions of classes, most people identify themselves based on the job that they have rather than by their social class. Jorrat proposes different aggregations for the development of five social classes:
- Services class, which includes managers and professionals of high-, middle-, and lower-command positions
- Routine non-manual workers, which comprise administrative employees in industrial and commercial activities related to both tangible goods and services
- Petty bourgeoisie, which includes artisans, farmers, and tenant farmers
- Skilled manual workers and manual workers' supervisors
- Unskilled manual workers

This common stereotype ticks almost all the boxes in my parents' case. They are immigrants from Galicia. My dad was a waiter first and then became the maintenance head of the building where I lived with him, with them, with my father and my mother, since I am an only child. He had that job for 46 years. Both of them worked hard and always saved money and wanted the best for their kid. They made every effort to give me everything they couldn't have. (P14, May 2020)

Most of the managers interviewed spoke about their families' opinions and mention the effort that they had made so that new generations could access education. These managers considered this an inspiration and aspiration as regards social values and believe that new generations must take it into account. Such values are viewed favorably by companies and revolve around sacrifice, perseverance, hard work, full dedication to work, effort, consistency, tenacity, saving capacity, and constant improvement. Thus, they represent moral assets to what these families understand as meritocracy and the development of a good life. From the interviewees' perspective, these are the desired qualities for people to develop projects as citizens of Argentina, and they become key elements when managers need to make highly crucial and difficult personal and professional decisions.

The interviewed female executives point out that women face more significant limitations as regards their professional careers, their university careers, their families, the language that they use, and even motherhood due to social or biological factors. P5, for example, states that her desire to pursue a professional career and the choice thereof were inspired by the only professional woman in her family. That woman set an example that motivated her to obtain a degree in public accountancy. She could visualize being independent and having monetary autonomy, in opposition to the case of other close relatives and even her mother, who were more focused on raising their children and working at home.[9]

---

[9]One vital issue as regards the differences in career choices refers to *"gender stereotypes."* Gender stereotypes are acquired during the learning processes, which are deeply influenced by the interaction with the most immediate social model— families and even schools—as well as cultural factors common to the society as a whole. When it comes to choosing university programs and professions, there are still social stereotypes regarding what is proper and improper for women to

After finishing high school, 3 of the 11 interviewees had their first work experiences in family businesses, businesses of their own, or SMEs (in Argentina known as PyMEs) owned by people trusted by their families. They were office assistants in banks or other public entities or performed simple administrative tasks. Some chose, on the other hand, to combine their university career development with other passions of theirs. It is essential to point out that, at this time, these women cared a lot about their families' opinion.

P6, for example, faced various stereotypes in her youth that ultimately shaped her final career decision.[10] She remembers that, when she finished high school, she was attracted to social careers, such as psychology and diplomacy, as well as to more technical careers, such as architecture and engineering. In fact, she liked architecture the most, but, during several conversations with her father and a male cousin of hers who was an engineer, she was criticized for wanting to obtain a degree in architecture since it was not a very *"feminine"* career.

As a result, she obtained a degree in English Teaching at the Higher Education Institute "Lenguas Vivas," since she considered that she was a natural—she used to play teacher when she was a child. But it was not actually a *"truly fulfilling"* profession for her. Her engineer cousin would argue that the downside of being an architect was that *"on one hand, there is no work because nothing is being built and, on the other, in the case of women.... Think of a pregnant woman going to the construction set"* (P6, May 2020). These remarks and comments by her family influenced,

---

do which directly affect their career choices and also foster the development of a labor market that continues to discriminate against women (OIT 2019).

[10]The hierarchical structure of the labor market is a social space where traditional gender roles are reproduced. Women are particularly affected because this structure is governed by strongly traditional parameters of distribution of individuals' activities by gender, which imposes profound restrictions on women's opportunities to access paid jobs. In this sense, Laura Pautassi (2013) points out that the increase in women's participation in the labor market must lead to the reflection on families' need to have another monetary income and be able to access basic resources. Previously, Elizabeth Jelin and Gustavo Paz. (1991) studied the increase in female participation in Latin America's labor force and pointed out that income is affected by pay discrimination and hiring practices are subject to the categorization of tasks and jobs as *"feminine"* and *"masculine."*

to a certain extent, her decision to move from more "*masculine*" professional careers to professional careers that had traditionally had more female participation. This is a stereotyped gender construct[11] related to the behaviors expected from each gender.

First Steps into the Managerial Path

Eight out of the eleven leaders interviewed began working directly for large private companies or providing services for them while pursuing their university studies. This allowed them to get familiar with the business world and have direct access to corporate information and different organizational cultures with the aim of either starting to gain experience and forge a corporate career or generating income to pay for their university studies.

Those women who were looking for a job resorted to the university's job bank, started a family business to continue the work carried out by their families, established their own business, or applied for jobs that they found in newspaper ads in order to access their first corporate job. They alternated between morning and evening classes and had full-time jobs. Many point out that a key element at this stage was learning to manage time and use the hours available to study—which many did at night—in an efficient way. Working and studying at the same time allowed them to apply what they learned at university in real jobs and, thus, to obtain a more comprehensive education as well as greater visibility and corporate responsibility. From the beginning of the professional career, and as I point out in the following chapters, "*time*" is considered a good that should be truly valued and invested rationally and efficiently.

When beginning her professional career, one of the managers interviewed started working on a project of her own, while the other 10 decided to join SMEs or work in junior positions at large companies. This

---

[11]The stereotyped construction of genders around society's beliefs or thoughts regarding men's and women's behaviors and abilities are acquired in a learning process influenced by cultural, community, and social behaviors giving rise to models that are reflected on family dynamics and institutions such as schools or companies.

group of executives began their careers by means of internships or young professional training programs. One of the first challenges they had to face early in their careers was not having a network of contacts to help them propel their management careers. P11 points out that, despite her father being a merchant who had not completed secondary school, he was the one who taught her the values and commercial aspects that prompted her to develop her career selling different business units.

Many women claim that the knowledge gained at university is used by companies in different business formats and circumstances. At the same time, they stress the importance of continuing to study and acquiring tools to differentiate themselves in the labor market. All the interviewees emphasize that it is essential to complement their hard skills, and the technical knowledge provided by undergraduate degrees with different seminars or postgraduate courses. Since postgraduate studies coincided with the times dedicated to their jobs, many managers opted for courses that would help them face new challenges in their professional careers, such as human resources, leadership, economics, and marketing. Some companies offer training programs, but many of them do not, so professionals *"have to cope by looking for useful tools on their own"* (P7, May 2020).

P1 started to work in companies where teams were made up of few women and where women did not occupy leadership positions. She decided to take different international exams, such as the TOEFL and the GMAA. She then obtained an MBA at Harvard University in Boston, United States, in order to differentiate herself and be able to access companies that had an inclusive organizational culture, shared her values, and offered an attractive professional career plan that would allow her to move up the company ladder in a short period of time.

P2's boss suggested her to obtain her master's degree at the Business School of IDEA (Institute of Business Development in Argentina), and she applied despite not meeting the age and experience requirements. Her goal was to work on her soft management skills, which were beneficial to move up the company ladder.

Among the testimonies of the managers interviewed, there are some exceptional cases of women whose work led them to choose their professional careers when they decided to start a second university program while continuing their professional development in a certain organization. P7 remembers that time as a moment of great physical and mental demand regarding her professional development.

> *It was like time-consuming. My time was only related to my work and my studies. The difference is that, when I was working full-time, work began to have more importance.*" (P7, May 2020)

Determination and the search for growth opportunities are features that the interviewees deem necessary to develop and gain experience in their management careers. They pointed out that being determined to continue learning in the organization, as well as understanding opportunities and different business units, allows for building trust and generating professional relations with company members who can become strategic allies when seeking internal growth in the company.

The Rise of Management Development

As regards their management careers, the leaders interviewed followed one of two paths.[12] One of them refers to the professional development in different companies, changing jobs for ones of higher hierarchy and accumulating different experiences.

The other alludes to the development of management careers in mainly one company, moving up the company ladder and gaining responsibilities when promoted. In both cases, as Florencia Luci (2016) points out, being a manager is the result of a process in which the professional identity and the class position associated with such job are constantly at stake.

---

[12]Professional development in different companies is part of a promotion and personal development strategy that allows managers to learn and acquire skills from different leadership styles and companies. Defillippi and Arthur (1994) studied cases in which managers became professionals trained in specific companies due to their "*know-why*" (organizations' commitment to more valuable professionals), their "*know-how*" (set of accumulated skills and experience), and their "*know-whom*" (importance of mentoring relationships in management careers within one specific organization).

Reaching a certain management position results from successfully navigating a career that involves strong competition; if the rank is higher, the positions are fewer" (Luci 2016, 118). The age when professionals are offered promotions in their management careers is also crucial; managers should be offered their first hierarchical position before turning 30. (Luci 2016)

In addition, both types of management careers share one relevant trait: occupying a regional position in another country. In the case of female managers, family planning and development constitute a relevant turning point in their professional and personal lives. Changes arising therefrom affect the development of routines, and the need to attend to both family and professional life requires a lot of organization and changes the lives of female managers and their families.

Two of the women interviewed developed their management careers in different companies, obtaining hierarchical promotions in different positions and business units until they were offered their current position as CEOs. Two executives developed their careers in different companies, but their most significant professional milestones took place in one specific company that caused their hierarchical rise to their current position.

Six of the women interviewed developed their management careers in one specific company or organization, moving up the ladder, being accompanied by company leaders and heads, and acquiring comprehensive knowledge of the organizational culture and the different business units until they were offered the position that they currently hold. Three of the interviewees started their management careers in companies that were sold or bought by other companies, which entailed changes in leadership styles and business cultures and which, at the same time, allowed for professional and hierarchical development in positions and business units that these managers found incredibly interesting.

P3, P4, and P8 experienced company mergers by the purchase and sale of business units. Some testimonies point out that mergers of companies of specific industries give professionals the opportunity to lead various projects. However, and at the same time, this requires more involvement in the politics of the corporate world, which can be complicated to face at the beginning of management careers. Taking into account these testimonies, two antagonistic views regarding company mergers can be noted.

P8 experienced company mergers throughout her entire management career, and, thus, she stresses the importance of acquiring experience and training within companies. She also mentions the benefits of leaving the *"comfort zone"* and getting involved in the various aspects of businesses as well as in other areas and with different clients, especially at moments of company purchases and sales and working with different teams and bosses.

She experienced constant mergers and acquisitions until she started working in the company where she currently works. Although mergers are much more common now, they used to be situations that generated tension and uncertainty regarding workers' job stability and their ability to adapt to new work dynamics and teams.

P8 began her career in a small national company acquired by a regional SME who was, in turn, acquired by three different multinational companies: one with British capital, one with Australian capital, and one with Swiss capital. She admits that the most significant challenges in her management career refer to interacting with people and developing teams, having to find appropriate profiles, understanding dynamics within each team, and balancing good ideas with individual feelings as well as the challenges faced by the company.

> *Moments when you are doing well and moments when you are doing poorly and you have to sell.... At the beginning, the first operations or the first negotiations to sell a company cause a lot of stress and a lot of fear in the team.... You have to help them see the positive side of the situation whether they continue working in the company or not. Every situation always gives you an opportunity and opens a new door.* (P8, May 2020)

On the other hand, P4 considers that a turning point in her professional life refers to the sale of an international bank's significant business unit after she had spent a large part of her professional career managing retail banking segments. This moment was crucial in her management career since she was in charge of a large team and had to deal with uncertainties regarding the employment situation of many people. At the same time, she was confident that bank buyers were interested in her profile.

One of the most prominent difficulties that these managers experienced was understanding the different stages of their professional development and recognizing the appropriate moment to change companies in pursuit of their professional and personal growth. The vast majority of female executives reached a point in their management careers when, after several years of growing and working in a certain company, they truly believed that they were going to retire there.

However, although there are specific reasons for changing companies or management career paths, more general aspects can be also analyzed, such as countries' economic crises, global economic crises, the need to change projects based on professional preferences, the opportunity of hierarchical and professional growth, and the persistent presence of the "*glass ceiling*," which will be addressed later on.

Where Do You Want to Raise Your Children and Where Do You Want to Die?

In 2018, the consulting firm Mercer carried out a study claiming that only 14 percent of the expatriate workforce are women, even though there has been some progress in this regard. Reaching the top management levels of multinational companies requires having international management experience as well as experience in managing projects and teams from other countries. In the aforementioned study, the low percentage of women expatriates in companies is accounted for by the fact that they are often discriminated against and disqualified or unsuccessful in their international management careers given the lack of corporate policies to help them as regards their families' relocation and support.

These issues are clearly present in the four cases of people assuming regional positions that I analyze below. Even though each of them goes through this process in a different way, all agree on the importance of being sure about certain values and professional goals as well as on the impact of these situations on family life.

P1 considers that working in different private investment funds and international holding companies allowed her to meet top-level directors and managers. These experiences and projects led her to the job that she had for nine years in one of the country's most influential management consulting firms. She was responsible for the coordination of a team of approximately 35 people in offices in Buenos Aires, Argentina, and Santiago de Chile, Chile.

Regarding her professional challenges, she was in charge of developing a skeptical industry's business brand following the events that took place in the 1990s, when the Argentine market resorted and paid large budgets to several consulting companies for projects that could not be implemented due to the Argentine 2001 economic crisis.

She points out that, as a result, developing a client portfolio involved a lot of dedication and effort. On the other hand, even though consultancy is much more popular in the Chilean market than in Argentina, she still needed to consider the competition and Chileans' loyalty to local companies. In addition, she had to face yet another challenge: being an Argentine woman and having to deal with generational barriers, gender barriers, and corporate culture barriers.

And Chileans are very localist, so hiring a Brazilian consultant in Chile is not easy, especially if a woman has to sell the idea, and most especially if that woman is Argentine. In that sense, Chile posed a great challenge. (P1, March 2020)

Adler (1995) points out that there is a construction of myths[13] and obstacles around the potential of female managers to expatriate and manage teams in other countries that is difficult to disregard. In general, men decide on the candidates who are offered international positions, and,

---

[13]Nancy Adler (1995) was one of the first researchers to investigate the reason why companies seem reluctant to promote women to positions abroad. In her research, she identifies three great myths:

Myth 1: Women are not interested in international positions in other countries.

Myth 2: Companies are reluctant to offer international courses or projects to women.

Myth 3: Prejudices against women in foreign cultures adversely affect their effectiveness in conducting and developing international projects.

thus, women are believed not to be interested in these positions. Moving to another country to develop a management career requires a lot of planning and responsibility both when making the decision and when facing its consequences.

Finally, September 11 attacks in New York, United States, and their consequences on the world and businesses altered P9's plans to move to the company's offices in Spain. She had requested such transfer since she wanted to move to Europe with her German husband, given that he had already lived in Argentina for several years. When the position in Spain opened up, she thought that she could expatriate without damaging her management career.

Nevertheless, the global business impairment made the company cancel her transfer to Spain. P9 still wanted to live in Europe and was able to continue her professional development in an encrypted telecommunications company that was part of a European business cluster with several business units. However, despite having some economic and professional stability, she decided to return to Argentina in 2004 to the same company where she had worked before moving.

Deciding to move to Europe and then returning to Argentina was one of the most complicated decisions that she had to face, as different pros and cons had to be considered in each moment. It was a question by a colleague manager what helped her decide to move back to Argentina. He asked her, "*Where do you want to die?*"

P4 started to work in the young professional's program of a bank, but, since she already had previous professional experience, she was offered a manager position within a short time. During this period, she had to face various decisions regarding both her professional career and her personal life; the dichotomy between developing a management career and a private affective life was always present. She stresses the importance of knowing her objectives and the kind of life that she wanted.

> *I always knew what I wanted. I like working. Working is exciting for me; it's not a burden.… But, throughout my career, I knew very well that, if I wanted to continue growing, there were personal decisions that I would have to make or postpone making.* (P4, April 2020)

One of the most important decisions in her life was deciding whether to develop professionally in a position abroad or not. She states that, at the beginning of her career, she put her personal life and her partner before her job and decided not to accept any positions abroad.

At a later moment of her management career, she realized that her desire to grow professionally was affecting her personal life and becoming a burden. After working in the Marketing, Product, and Planning departments, she decided to take a regional position, which was a crucial moment in her career. She believes that couples cannot be solely blamed when a partner's professional development and the couple's goals are not balanced. After this experience, she decided to return to the business in Argentina and focus on her personal life and her husband. She started therapy in order to reflect and work on those aspects sacrificed for the development of her professional career.

You can't blame anyone, it's what you decide for yourself. And, in perspective, I somehow put my personal life on hold because I was on a plane every day, working hours and hours, dedicating a lot to the office.... But, when you think about it, I don't know if you are so aware of that at the moment. (P4, April 2020)

P6 had a very different experience living abroad. When she received the job offer from the global team of the industrial company where she was working, her first maternity leave was about to end, and she was also on the verge of finishing her master's thesis. The global team analyzed her business unit's exponential growth and local developments as well as their strategic alliances and partnerships.

Two months after her meeting with the global VPs, she received an offer to attend a leadership course and a Master Black Belt[14] in a division in

---

[14]Master Black Belt represents a high level of experience and responsibility in the strategic deployment of the Six Sigma methodology—a strategy to improve business processes by controlling variation, reinforcing and optimizing each part thereof, and reducing or eliminating defects or failures in the delivery of products or services to customers—within an organization. The main purpose is to promote and support activities in order to improve all company's commercial and operational areas, as well as suppliers and customers, thus attending to all the parties involved in the projects.

the United States. This was a crucial moment in her management career since it is not common to be offered such position and many factors had to be considered before accepting it. She is an only child and was always in charge of her parents, who, at the same time, were her support network and helped taking care of her daughter.

> *I received this offer when I wasn't ready. I wasn't prepared to leave my parents, I wasn't prepared to leave my daughter in a daycare center away from her grandparents. And I found out that I was pregnant with my second daughter when I had already rented a house there. We talked about it with my husband. We had a job here and we also had help to take care of our daughter. My husband had friends, a life, a job ... and we were leaving.* (P6, May 2020)

She remembers that she had to look for an obstetrician as soon as she arrived in the United States. She was living two completely opposite moments at the same time. On a professional level, despite the difficulties in her family and her private life, she was able to undergo many learning experiences. However, on a personal level, having two young daughters posed many challenges regarding their daily organization; cultural, parenting, and care differences with their nanny; relocation stress; and family conflicts.

Since her husband could not find a job, the relationship between them was tense.[15] After a year and a half, she was offered a global marketing position that allowed her to continue learning. Finally, in 2009, two years after moving abroad, she had to decide whether to keep that global position or return to Argentina. At the same time, the whole family went through a situation that would prove to be decisive: Her youngest daughter had a household accident. She fell and underwent a skull surgery, so P6 decided to return to Argentina.

She accepted a job, and, after her transfer to Argentina was concluded, she found out that it was a lower position in a minor business division, which represented a setback in her professional career.[16] It was

---

[15]The interviewee's tone of voice became more nervous and serious.
[16]The interviewee showed anger and sadness.

an extremely complicated decision to make, and she was deeply upset at the time, so she decided to change the course of her management career. She describes what she felt as *"pain of the soul."*[17] As a result of these experiences and the feeling that her management career was in decline, she decided to contact a colleague who worked in the consulting world to discuss possible new options. At that moment, she was offered a position in an important company selling mass consumption products.

Given that, in most countries, the number of women in management positions is low, it is difficult for companies to suggest women professionals for international positions. Adler (1995) challenges the traditional belief that women do not aspire to have positions abroad or relocate. In fact, accepting a job offer abroad allows managers to gain skills that are very beneficial for their management career development because they acquire a global vision of business as well as the ability to work with diverse teams and adapt to different leadership styles.

Based on these testimonies, it can be now claimed that female managers resist or find it more difficult to expatriate and accept positions of greater responsibility in other countries mainly because they do not have a family supporting structure that eases their children's relocation. As a result, these women and their partners have to face all the challenges involved in this decision on their own.

It Is Not Enough to Have a Mentor—You Need a Sponsor

In this section, I will focus on the role of bosses, mentors, and sponsors in the professional development of female managers as facilitators regarding their promotion and integration in the highest ranks of organizational pyramids. Professionals pursuing management careers constantly seek new challenges that allow for professional growth and learning under different management and corporate styles. The interviewees emphasize the importance of knowing their professional values, and they also note the significance of developing in an environment sharing such values as well as being aware of the *"losses and gains"* involved in the decisions made at each management stage.

---

[17]The interviewee had to take a moment before continuing the interview.

The teachings of bosses and mentors as well as the internal and external networking opportunities help promote professional growth. In this way, professionals can make a name for themselves and receive positive references when they consider upward mobility. Bosses may be completely different: While some help develop the careers of rising professionals, many of them do not only refuse to help these professionals but also deliberately hinder their professional advancement.

The experiences of the professionals interviewed also vary greatly. Bosses must have a set of specific skills and abilities that they build throughout their management careers and that relate to the ability to teach and motivate teams as well as deal with their complex emotions. Regardless of their skills, leaders can decide to dedicate more time to teaching or motivating teams.

> *I had excellent bosses who supported me and helped me. Some thought about leaving their jobs at some point and used me; they helped me develop my career to tell others, "I already have someone to replace me. And it was useful for me too." (P2, March 2020)*

> *The truth is that I was very lucky throughout my career. All my male bosses were examples of leaders and fathers who managed to reconcile their personal and work life. So, regardless of their gender, they were very present dads. And that context becomes useful because you are actually working with leaders who are also very present dads.* (P9, May 2020)

Managers must learn from "*good bosses*" throughout their professional development and take into account the different qualities that can be applied in their own way of working in order to be ready to put them into practice when reaching leadership positions. Bosses directly impact teams' productive capacity, increasing individual productivity of workers and positively affecting the productive capacity of work teams and projects (Lazear et al. 2015). I will analyze bosses' impact on two women's management careers by considering those who were present throughout their professional development.

P2 began working in a company only three months after graduating from university. She claims that bosses' support to professionals' careers as well as each person's ability and search for continuous learning opportunities are critical aspects as regards women's management development. In her case, this led her to become the Leader of Personnel Administration and Recruitment; then, the Manager of Compensations and Benefits; and, after that, the Manager of Human Resources for the Southern Cone, a position that she held for 18 years until she became part of the Human Resources Management and Presidency.

Machiavelli is an inspiration to P10 when she reflects on her management career. She started her management career in a junior position and was then offered an important promotion because the coordinator left the organization and the manager of such area was about to retire. She became Coordinator and, a few years later, she took on the position of Manager. "*Machiavelli states that the prince must have virtue and fortune, and I think that there was a bit of both in my career*" (P10, July 2020).

She believes that one can build "*virtue*" by committing to the organization, being curious about the operational logics of the business structure, and being open to learning from superiors. In her opinion, building virtue depends on each professional's attitude and on the generosity of those working with her. If she had not had bosses who would share their skills and their way of thinking when solving different situations, she would not have been able to acquire the skills necessary for her job. On the other hand, the dimension of chance that Machiavelli calls "*fortune*" refers to the circumstances that lead you to be in the right place when specific opportunities arise.

She remembers that the situation when she was offered her management position was really exceptional. She actually had to replace a woman who had been in that position for 20 years, and P10 had not even turned 30. In fact, she became the youngest manager and the only female manager in an organization with deep gender and generational gaps.

Her first year in such position was truly challenging due to the high employee turnover: The Logistics Manager, the Deputy Logistics Manager, and the Head of Administration resigned, and the Administration Manager was fired. As a result, it was more difficult for her to carry out the innovation management process that she had planned. Fortunately, one of her bosses supported her new ideas and helped her implement them. Taking on a management position at a very young age made her consider her continuity at the organization. She considered if she wanted to have a leadership position at such a young age and decided to take one more year and see if she can really do it.

During their professional careers, the interviewed managers also had bosses who were not honest or transparent. They came across bosses who did not support their teams, who were mediocre in their jobs, and who were not born leaders. However, they also worked with bosses who were great leaders and who inspired them professionally.

Andrés Hatum, a professor at Torcuato Di Tella University (UTDT), analyzes the characteristics of "*bad bosses*": bosses who seize their teams' achievements, who do not have teaching or motivational skills, and who are even abusive. These bosses affect the development of organizations and professional teams, damaging the company's values, causing talent loss, and putting the company's long-term sustainability at risk (Hatum 2020). However, despite these experiences, both female managers decided not to change companies.

When P7 was appointed Manager and, then, Management Director, she began a new arduous learning process. Due to the organization's structure, there were few managers to learn from and she faced a "*trial and error*" process, which gave rise to conflicts and hostilities with some people in the company. "*That was the first confrontation I had, and I didn't do it very well because I was inexperienced, I think. I wouldn't do things the same way today*" (P7, May 2020). She claims that there was no one to support her and help her face these new challenges—neither inside nor outside the organization—and, hence, she found the job lonely.

> So, it was a difficult first confrontation and I faced lots of long faces and bad moods, and lots of my ideas were rejected, and I made lots of mistakes. It was difficult. (P7, May 2020)

When a new CEO was appointed and teams were reorganized, she had some conflicts because she became tired of proposing ideas that were never implemented. In addition, gender-related distinctions and confrontations between men and women were commonplace in the company, and P7 experienced these situations firsthand in respect to her male boss. She was much younger than him and had a very different education. However, their relationship changed given the results of her work and the appointment of the current female Director of Finance. Her boss then asked her to stay and continue developing her management career in that organization.

P5 was the fourth female executive in the company, but her appointment was made official three years after she commenced exercising her duties. During her career, she had the chance of changing jobs every three years. First, she started working as an intern for a young professionals' program and, thus, coordinated a call center locally and regionally, and also in Spain, the United States, and Latin America. When she returned to her position in Argentina, she was in charge of a team in which only 3 percent of the members were women. Coordinating this team was a significant challenge as regards project development: She even remembers crying in the car after the workday was over—she did not want to be seen crying in the company so as not to lose her authority and her colleagues' respect.

The CEO change in 2012 was a crucial moment in her management career because the new CEO decided to incorporate several people who he trusted and who caused problems in many business units. The biggest challenge was reconciling the different Human Resources management decisions that were made by the company's two most important business units. One business unit was managed informally—not by the corporate management—while the other worked hand in hand with the company's Human Resources department.

At that time, her appointment as executive had not been made official yet, and she felt that the company was facing a considerable ethical dilemma, so she decided, along with three other professionals, to resign. The CEO, as a result, set a meeting with her and asked her the reasons why she had made such decision. He was unaware of the way in which the company was being run and its effect on business procedures and transparency and, thus, claimed that she resigned because her appointment had not been made official. She remembers, in an angry manner, such conversation as stated below:

And he says, "You can't go. You're leaving because we didn't make you executive." And I said that wasn't the case and that I'd already forgotten about that because I knew they were never going to do it. If that had been the reason, I'd have left three years before. I just disagreed with how things were being handled. (P5, May 2020)

After her conversation with the CEO and their exchange of views on the future of business units' management, she decided to continue working in the company and was officially appointed executive. She also took on responsibilities as regards institutional matters and continued carrying out projects and growing professionally.

The interviewees consider it essential for professionals to have mentors and sponsors to help boost their management careers. It is also important for them to learn how to network with other professionals and how to make themselves known at events and in the business world by building solid relations. One of the executives interviewed alludes to her personal experience regarding her management growth and her sponsor's support.

I always say that you don't need a mentor in a company: you need a sponsor. I mean, you do need a mentor, but, to continue growing, you need a sponsor. A mentor just tells you where to go, but that doesn't take you anywhere. If you don't have a sponsor, a person calling the shots and helping you actually get there, you can't make it, even if you are the very best. (P11, July 2020)

Both mentors and sponsors commit to the development of professionals because they can see their potential. Moreover, they can achieve political and economic benefits as well as greater business development thanks to these professionals' progress and hard work. "*Mentors and sponsors like what you do; they think what you do is good and that it adds value to their own work*" (P11, July 2020). Professional networking is essential for job advancement and promotions, especially in management or leadership positions, since the direct exchange with others and the social capital arising therefrom make a difference in managers' performance.

In this sense, the interviewees stressed the importance of networking with other professionals in the same company as well as in other companies and making themselves known at corporate events and in the business world by building solid relationships. This symbolic sense of community helps build professional relations that can lead to benefits and incentives in their professional careers (Luci 2009).

Sponsors value and believe in professionals. They guide them in the business world, help develop their social and political relations, and promote their access to negotiation and decision-making processes. If professional managers are capable of learning from mentors and sponsors' experiences, they will eventually reap the rewards of their dedication of time and resources. As a result of the research made here for, it can be now claimed that female managers need the support of bosses, mentors, and, especially, sponsors to move up the company ladder and be included in decision making and networking spaces where socializing and business take place.

What Is Hidden in Plain Sight, in the Managerial Career?

Throughout their management careers, all the professionals interviewed reported having faced discrimination and/or gender stereotypes, whether they were aware of it or not. Even though some of them first stated otherwise, I could spot some experiences in that respect in all the testimonies. Moreover, as the interviews continued, the interviewees were able to reflect on certain situations experienced as well as their own discourse and recognized instances of discrimination, sexism, obstacles in their career paths, and even harassment. This was possible because we had developed a trust relation that allowed them to talk openly about these issues.

Even some of the men interviewed openly referred to certain job benefits that allowed them to spend more time with their families and that derived from male stereotypes regarding their role in the upbringing of their children.

The experiences lived by these executives are diverse and will be illustrated with examples. We discussed certain problems related to gender-based discrimination faced during their careers as professionals on the rise and then as team leaders, directors, and CEOs. Certain matters common to all cases are included below (Figure 7):

Sexist Comments

- Disregard or invalidation of their decisions based on their alleged lack of experience: "Come here, darling. I'll explain it to you."
- Comments on women's mood.
- Typification of women's behaviors as nervous or hysterical.
- Comments on the bodies of female colleagues or famous women.

Exclusion from Conversations due to Gender

- Conversations about football, golf, and other sports.
- Underrepresentation of women in meetings, which leads to them being excluded from conversations. Women's fear and worry about actively participating in meetings with mostly men who also socialize outside the workplace.

Salary Gap and Moving Up the Ladder

- Lower salaries than male colleagues.
- Challenge of working in their teams and in executive processes.
- Creation of intermediate positions.
- Longer trial periods.
- Unofficial positions.

Taking Time Off to Be with Their Families

- Gender stereotypes regarding women's and men's roles in their families.
- The importance thereof as regards public and corporate policies.

Harassment

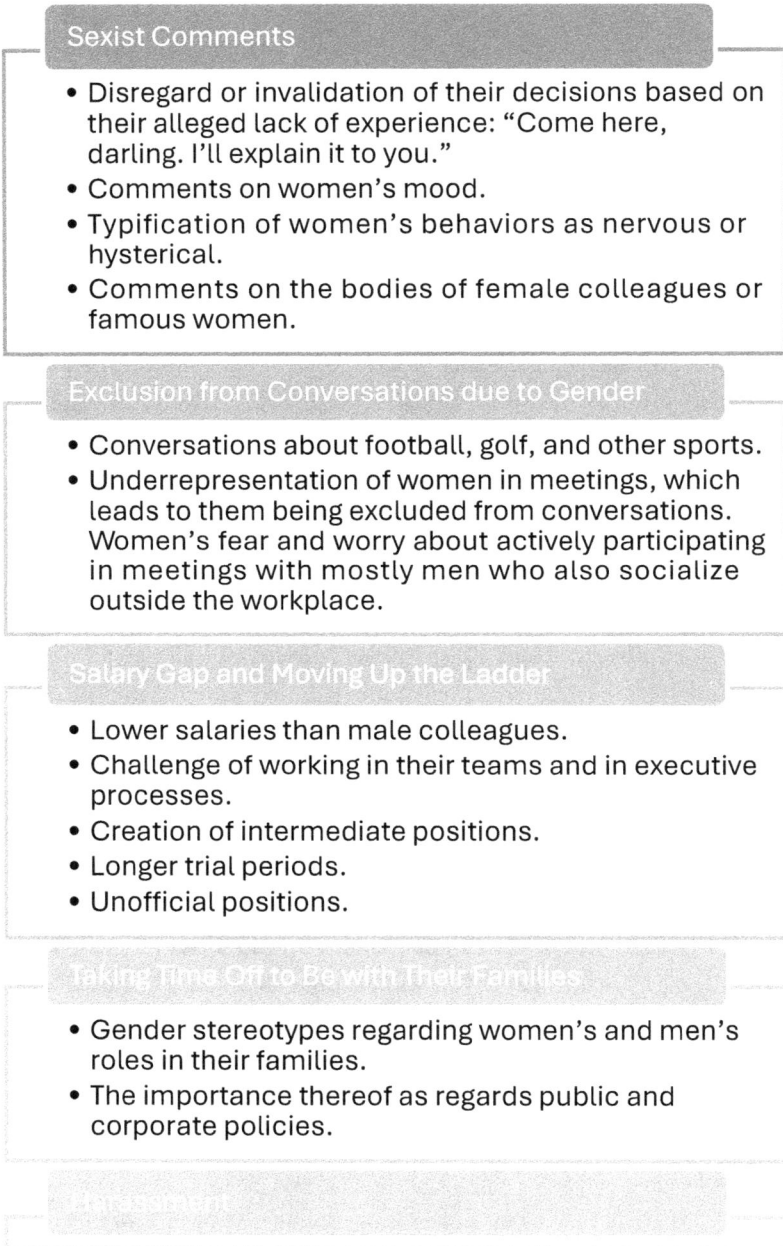

Figure 7 Female Managers' Experience with Discrimination

In the light of the aforementioned, each situation will be analyzed taking into account the interviewees' testimonies regarding how their professional careers were affected.

¿Por qué no te tomas un tecito?—Why Don't You Have a Cup of Tea?[18]

Six of the female executives interviewed—that is to say, more than half of the interviewees—experienced situations involving sexist, politically incorrect, and uncomfortable comments related directly to their gender. These comments were disguised as opinions at negotiation tables or were actually more personal attacks during business discussions. In addition, four of the interviewed managers claim that the most significant obstacles faced as regards negotiations and relationships with peers and bosses were directly linked not only to being women but also to their age and, in some cases, to holding leadership positions at very young ages in comparison to other managers in the organization.

According to the 2016 ILO report "Young and Female—A Double Strike?," the gender analysis of school-to-work transition surveys of 32 developing countries reveals that young women are more exposed to discrimination when they start their management careers, which reinforces inequality. Such discrimination starts as horizontal segregation (high representation of women in specific productive sectors and professions, strictly based on gender stereotypes) and vertical segregation (women's actual possibility of moving up the company ladder). However, the

---

[18]The Argentine expression "tomate un tecito" is a colloquial way of saying "relax" or "calm your nerves." "Tecito" is a diminutive form of "tea." The expression "Why don't you have a cup of tea?" in the context of business in Argentina may have additional connotations. While it is still an invitation to relax and take a break, it can also convey a tone of paternalism or sexism, depending on the context and who is saying it.

In some situations, it may be perceived as a condescending comment or one that minimizes a woman's professional abilities, implying that she should calm down or relax as if she were less able to handle the pressure than a man in the same situation.

It is important to consider the tone and context in which this expression is used, as it can vary greatly depending on who says it and how it is said.

educational background, such as having a master's degree or an MBA, allows women to be able to decide to work in companies and teams—and even with bosses—sharing their values; education places them in a privileged position.

When P2 worked in factories, she had to face a double challenge: being a woman and being very young. She worked with people who were much older than her and who sometimes did not fully consider her professional contributions. Likewise, women often face these challenges both inside and outside the organization. Given the business where P2 worked, her age became a clear problem when she began to work with unions, which are organizations historically occupied by older men. She had to face comments such as *"Come here, darling. I'll explain it to you,"* which evidence the aforementioned double inequality deriving from being a woman and being young.

The interviewees argue that it is necessary to start learning from the very beginning of management careers to take part in negotiation tables in order to understand very male-dominated situations and, as a result, get one's point across. Likewise, P2 believes that these situations can be better handled if young professionals have bosses who support their careers, teach them, and value their vision and contributions. Women consider that the best way to deal with these comments is not to take them personally and, instead, to focus on the professional goals. This clearly evidences the normalization of daily sexist and vulgar comments as well as the stereotype of *"female hysteria."* P6 even argues that these comments contribute to the development of alliances and strategies since, in fact, professionals gain experience from harsh conversations with colleagues. She points out that learning to have some coffee and talk directly with more aggressive professionals[19] allows professionals to break down prejudice barriers and to test themselves in different situations, subsequently building trust relations.

---

[19]Lamas (2021) claims that gender stereotypes as well as women's and men's roles and qualities are established through the construction process of society's symbolic order. Thus, if women's and men's social roles are defined symbolically, they are collective cultural constructions, just like the hierarchies determining the role of each person in society. Symbolically, as a result, sexual differences translate into power differences, which generally lead to different types of conflicts.

If you manage to be valued for your inputs, because people always have something to chip in because nobody gets anywhere if they don't, then men end up telling you, "Relax, dude." So, it's about trying to get there. (P6, May 2020)

Even in higher positions and small boards of directors, women have to bear politically incorrect comments during tense negotiations or exchanges. Reaching a small board of directors or executive committee, where women are underrepresented and often only one of them takes part, is to start a new career from the very beginning, and this difficulty is not always considered (IDEA 2018). As many as 10 out of the 11 CEOs interviewed claim that it is tough to be the only woman in management, sometimes among executives who they have worked with for years.

Hence, they feel forced to tolerate comments such as *"you need a cup of tea"* or *"you are being a bit nervous,"* which are linked to the hysteria or nervousness typically associated with women who stand for themselves in discussions or exchanges. These comments respond to the stereotype of female leaders being more emotional.

In this sense, Ramos et al. (2003) refer to Loden's work—*Feminine Leadership or How to Succeed in Business Without Being One of the Boys* (1987)—on feminine and masculine corporate leadership styles. The authors focus on a feminine leadership style instead of the traditional masculine one and center on feminine qualities. In this sense, it is claimed that the feminine-natural management style is based on rational as well as emotional issues, and, thus, it fosters the building of cooperative relations and places importance on the well-being and development of teams.

Female managers tend to build closer personal relations with their teams and consider both rational and emotional factors when making decisions, looking for solutions in which all parties involved get some benefits and a certain level of satisfaction (Ramos et al. 2003). This is a distinctive characteristic of the more feminine form of leadership, which can be contrasted with most men's approach, which is more goal-oriented than process-oriented.

Only two of the women interviewed acknowledge having faced sexist comments from peers and/or bosses during their professional careers. The executives interviewed argue that the way in which women are talked to and treated in companies has changed. In this regard, the experiences of two CEOs and their response are included below. One of them was the marketing coordinator in a significant industrial company.

She mentions that she was very young and that her career was just starting and, thus, felt uncomfortable when hearing her male colleagues comment on women's bodies and models' curves—even just before formal meetings—and engage in homophobic conversations and other types of conversations that were normalized at that time. Today, such comments are not so common, and conversations with other professionals and colleagues are much more careful.

> *Sometimes they'd start talking about some woman's ass and commented on models' butts before meetings, and it was a bit awkward.... I don't know, I didn't feel the same way.... It was difficult for me to know where to stand.... They had homophobic conversations that were horrifying. Maybe not on purpose, but I tended to blush, do you get me?* [I did get her] *They'd laugh and make fun of me.* (P6, May 2020)

On the other hand, the second manager worked in the oil industry, which is, in her opinion, a very sexist industry. She remembers that many men took women—other than their wives—to camps in oil towns. Such industry, she claims, used to place women in a less professional role, and was forced to rapidly transform and adapt to changes in the labor market.

> *I'm not talking about 60-year-old men. I'm talking about men who are now 50 years old, who were new professionals 25 years ago and who could have treated girls differently.* (P5, April 2020)

In her opinion, women in the said industry necessarily have to prove that they are up to other professionals' level. As a result, they generally end up becoming a masculine version of themselves. They work late, are not empathetic, avoid crying or expressing anguish and discontent in public, and are even cruel to other women who decide not to adopt this attitude. P5 points out that the oil industry is a particularly competitive industry, but general corporate rules still apply; getting promoted involves dedicating a lot of time to the business, having a strong personality, and showing no feelings or emotions. She was part of corporate boards made up of mainly men and witnessed extremely uncomfortable conversations about other women. She would put a smile on her face and not call them out because that could be detrimental to her.

"Women who now say "I didn't suffer any discrimination and I always worked with men… I say "Don't f..k with me. You adapted and you're probably quite a b..h towards other women now." (P5, April 2020)

The social construction of women being more collaborative, empathetic, kind, and understanding and relying more on other team members may be untrue in the case of some women and may be true in the case of some men. It can be argued that new leaderships require managers to acquire skills typical of both men and women. However, there are still daily micro-relations that perpetuate gender stereotypes and cause gender inequality between executives.

How to Find a Place Among So Many Men?

Four of the women interviewed claim that they are still excluded from conversations in large boards of directors and groups as well as networking spaces due to gender. There are more men than women present in meetings, and they usually talk about soccer and sports in general as well as women's bodies. These four women also claim that, many times, men change the topic of conversation when women are present and do not let them fully participate in discussions. In consequence, women feel uncomfortable because they are underrepresented in these situations and refrain from participating in meetings because they are not comfortable and are somewhat afraid to take part and share their point of view. Women have to take courage in order to actively participate and *"earn a seat"* at the executive table.

Many claim that women's participation and integration in these meetings is mainly hindered by women's underrepresentation therein (taking into account the number of women present in boards) and the time when they are held (very early in the morning or at the end of the day, which coincides with the time when women carry out care tasks). Female managers state that this is not necessarily discrimination, but they do claim that being a woman is different: Being a new man joining a space with mainly men is not the same as being a woman joining a space where less than 10 percent of its members are women.

I am a very courageous woman. I don't have problems with speaking in front of 10,000 people, I really don't mind. But sometimes I'd have breakfast alone or nearly alone, and my legs would shake, do you get my point? When I approached a table with so many men, they'd sometimes shut up not because I came in, but because they were talking about something that a woman should not hear. Sometimes I'd walk with other CEOs, and they would shut up when I came in, and you are like "fuck this," do you get me? They'd be talking either about football or girls. Those things happen and they're real. (P3, April 2020)

P11 is an expert on this subject and claims that, nowadays, women must change their mindset regarding these issues in order to reach leadership positions and integrate into executives' tables with mainly men. Female managers must adapt to male-dominated organizations to fit in and become part of them. They should try to foster their ambition, develop their own projects, and pay attention to the importance of networking and balancing work and family.

In this sense, the interviewees point out that ambition is a quality more associated with men than women. However, women should not see their professional developed hindered because they are forced to fight extremely harder in order to achieve their goals (Luci 2009).

Emotional agility is another important aspect that, in the interviewees' opinion, needs to be worked on so that it is not affected by management career development. Carrying out projects of one's own and showing entrepreneurial spirit is a way of developing a professional career, and, hence, professional women should carefully plan their management careers and clearly identify their objectives and the challenges involved in order to achieve their goals. Women need to start sharing and occupying the spaces dominated by men as well as mingling with workmates outside the office.

People don't need to network after office hours. You can do it from 9
to 6 and, if we ever have to do it after office hours, we can compensate
our kids at another time and ask our mom, our husband, the nanny,
or whoever to look after them and just go. Even women who don't
have children are not always present in these spaces because there're
few women and they decide not to go, and that's a mindset that has to
be changed. (F11, July 2020)

Many businesses are made outside office hours in different socialization spaces. The women interviewed acknowledge that they do not
usually engage in activities that take place after 6:00 p.m. because they
overlap with care and family activities. Some of the inequalities faced
by female managers derive from having to adapt to masculine structures
mainly dominated by men. Women have to seek ways to participate in
socialization activities that men have historically carried out after office
hours and that overlap with care and family life tasks.

The Climbing of the Company Ladder

Due to the labor market logics, it becomes difficult to clearly identify the
presence of certain elements. However, three of the women interviewed
claim having suffered gender-based pay discrimination. At certain moments of their management careers, these women had male colleagues
with equal responsibilities and seniority who earned higher salaries. All
the interviewees agree that companies and the national government must
continue developing public policies in search of real workplace equality.

I even disdained the idea of having children because I felt that being a
woman hadn't affected my growth. I've never resented being a woman.
I've been possibly paid less than men, I am sure that I was affected
by the salary gap, and I can also remember some situations of people
thinking I was an assistant or a secretary because I was young and
a woman. (P10, July 2020)

Magalí Brosio (2016) refers to data by the ILO indicating that, on
average, women earn approximately 27 percent less than men, taking into

account the difference between the average salary of men and women. She proposes considering further variables in her analysis, given that using only the aforementioned indicator disregards other four elements that directly impact the perpetuation of the pay gap. These elements are the following: the number of hours worked, vertical segregation (women's underrepresentation in leadership positions), horizontal segregation (distribution of women in the economic sectors), and unequal pay for equal qualifications.

P4 points out that her decision to leave one of her first jobs was mainly based on the company's decision to open a quota for only one woman chief, which conditioned the careers of the women who worked at the company and sought a job promotion. Addressing and being aware of the fact that maternity is usually an obstacle to management careers is also extremely challenging. Only two interviewees agree that motherhood implied not being able to move up the career ladder—or being given the opportunity once the maternity leave was over—as well as being offered promotions only to new intermediate positions.

On the one hand, there are cases such as P5's, who, being 36 years old, suffered gender discrimination at the time of her promotion to executive—when only three executives (aged 45 or older) were women. At that same time, a 39/40-year-old male professional was offered an official position as executive after six months of work, while P5 was promoted on a trial basis subject to her performance. She worked on trial for three years until she decided to resign, and, consequently, the company offered to make her position official so that she would continue working there. Despite achieving the best results, fulfilling demanding goals, and having the best performance in the company's human resources department, she could never be part of the executive board.

On the other hand, there are cases like P3's, who used to work in a Big Four[20] company and whose management career was affected when

---

[20]Big Four is the nickname used to collectively refer to the four largest professional consulting services firms in the world: Deloitte; Ernst & Young; KPMG; and PwC. They are grouped by company size (in relation to the rest of the market, both in terms of revenue and workforce) and the capacity to provide a wide range of professional services: auditing, assurance, tax, management, actuarial, finance, and legal services.

she became a mother. P3 became pregnant the year when she was going to be promoted to partner. As a result, the business partners assumed that maybe she was not ready to undertake all the responsibilities involved in the new position and, thus, created a brand-new position for her: Associate Director. She questioned such decision because she fulfilled all the requirements and had the skills necessary to become a partner. In her opinion, this qualifies as gender discrimination. The company itself admitted that P3 was, in fact, ready for a partner position but, instead, created a new intermediate position for her and offered such partner position again only a year later.

> *In these firms, you can be Manager, Senior Manager, or Partner. And when they had to make me a Partner, they made up this Director category and placed me there for one year. I was like: "Yes, great, thanks for the recognition, but you've invented this category for me because I'm a woman." Or, at least, that's what I thought at the time. And I told them so. (P3, April 2020)*

In the 2016 and 2017 studies, the ILO stressed the importance of promoting training, networking, consultancy, and the revision of management hiring and promotion systems in order to increase the number of women in management positions as well as to implement family-friendly policies, thus giving rise to more empathetic leadership and a more inclusive business culture. The research that I have carried out reveals the existence of gender-based pay inequality in the professional labor market and of obstacles that hinder women professionals' promotions in management careers, mainly in the light of motherhood. As a result, female managers "fall behind" in their careers and are unable to reach leadership positions.

Difficulties in Taking Maternity Leaves

P12, one of the male CEOs interviewed, agrees that companies have to update and work on corporate policies regarding maternity and paternity leaves, given men's and women's roles in children's upbringing.

I've promoted women that were on maternity leave to managers and senior managers. The leave period also has to count because, if not, women would be at a disadvantage. Many companies consider promoting women on leave when they come back, but that's not okay. I take them into account, and, if they are ready, I just promote them. (P12, May 2020)

P1 was responsible for interviewing candidates for the Head of Administration position. When she made a decision, the woman selected told her that, before accepting the position, she needed to confess that she was three months pregnant. P1 replied that she did not understand her point because that did not change her opinion about her job, her career development, or her qualifications. She realizes that, even today, women who want to start a family are not equally considered and the fear of being pregnant when applying for a new job or seeking a promotion is still very much present.

On the other hand, P13, another male CEO interviewed, comments on an interview that he had with a female professional who is currently part of his team. During such interview, such candidate told him that she had recently confirmed with her doctor that she was pregnant. P13 instinctively congratulated her and gave her a hug. The woman looked at him in surprise and said that she felt obligated to tell him about her pregnancy because she thought that he might decide not to hire her for that reason.

Even today, he finds it difficult to understand that women are often not hired because they are pregnant, but, in fact, this was not what surprised him the most. Later that day, he had a conversation with a female executive working in a multinational company who was aware of the abovementioned interview and who told him that she would not have hired a professional who was pregnant. Despite the opinions of the men interviewed, all the interviewed women strongly believe that, in fact, women face more problems than men when accessing new jobs, especially if positions involve moving up the management ladder, because companies are "afraid" that they may take time off if they become pregnant.

None of the women interviewed had problems requesting maternity leaves or other family leaves—sick children, school events, or other children-related situations. Maternity leaves will be analyzed in the next chapter. However, this chapter includes the case of P12, one of the men interviewed, who could not request paternity leaves nor vacation leaves to share time with his family. As a result, now that he has become the boss, he tries to always grant leaves to his team members because he feels very sorry for having missed activities and quality time moments with his family.

Having to sacrifice vacations and family activities, such as school events and health emergencies, due to the difficulties faced when requesting leaves deeply upsets him. He even considers this a career regret, since he will never be able to recover the time lost. Today, he encourages his team members to not only take vacation days and spend quality time with their families but to also continue working responsibly as a team in order to avoid neglecting work obligations. The research carried out therefore reveals that the male management career model adversely affects both women and men, who are forced to change their behavior and adapt to such system. Inequality stems from the fact that men feel more comfortable with such model because women are usually in charge of family and care structures. Therefore, and as the interviewees point out, women often end up experiencing gender-based discrimination.

Difficulties in Dealing with Harassment

Only one of the interviewees claims having experienced harassment during her management career. Whenever this topic was mentioned, the interviewees automatically replied that they had not been subject to harassment. They, however, mention knowing one or more professionals who underwent this type of situation. This was definitely the most difficult subject to address during the interviews. Nevertheless, as the interviews progressed, many of the interviewees realized that they may have experienced situations that are now defined as harassment but that used to be normalized and socially accepted. Harassment is difficult to spot.

Nevertheless, many claim that new generations have brought about many important changes: Discussions have become much more open, and society has begun denouncing certain behaviors. At the same time, however, some dread reaching a point where mixed-gender teams begin to disappear. P12, one of the male interviewees, claims that members of the team under his charge have experienced workplace and sexual harassment and states that, despite the situation's complexity, the only possible course of action is to impose sanctions.

Considering their current leadership roles and responsibilities, the interviewees agree that this issue is highly delicate and should be carefully addressed. In this sense, three of the interviewees claim having faced complex situations and mention that, nowadays, there is more awareness as well as more tools available to implement in order to take care of their teams.

CHAPTER 3

From CEO to Chief Executive Mom Officer

Despite the advances in the global labor market and the increase in the number of women participating in the formal labor market, in fact, few women currently lead big companies, hold government leadership positions, or occupy positions at the top of organizations in general. According to the data collected by ELA for the year 2020, only 20 percent of the highest political positions in the Argentine Executive and Legislative branches are occupied by women.

In other words, out of every 10 political positions, 8 are held by men and only 2 are held by women. Analyzing civil society organizations, which are more heterogeneous and employ more women, still only 35.9 percent of leadership positions are held by women. The situation is even more unequal in trade unions: Barely 5 percent of national unions have women at their executive committees. Furthermore, as regards media, less than 10 percent of the highest positions in open media companies are occupied by women.

In the Argentine business world, the situation is not very different in terms of occupation distribution since women hold approximately 4.4 percent of management positions in large companies (ELA 2021).

This chapter analyzes the life stage characterized by the women interviewed deciding whether to start a family or not, rearranging their available times, and using their own lives and experiences to think about the kind of managers that they wanted to be and that companies should have. At this point in life—between the age of 30 and 45—more importance is given to the social pressure concerning the motherhood mandate, starting a family, and fully developing in a management career.

The interviewees agree that being female managers at the top of their careers implies an enormous responsibility because they consider themselves role models for future generations. Being a female manager involves constant learning and pressures about balancing the management career and family life. Companies expect women to neglect neither of these when they become female leaders in a predominantly male universe that exposes them to criticism and opinions.

Many writings reveal the moral understanding of women's role in society and the reasons for such a view. On the one hand, women are sometimes thought not to have the innate psychological traits necessary to exercise reasonable and assertive leadership, thus lacking the skills and experience necessary to succeed a male leader. Women are often considered to lack ambition and desire for power and not to fight to access leadership positions (Peterson and Farrell 2018). These ideas may be associated with preconceptions historically built regarding men's and women's roles (ILO 2017a), but, today, women still receive contradictory advice throughout their management careers that contributes to these gender typifications. Women are supposed to be decisive and assertive as well as accessible and friendly.

They must be collaborative but not lose their credibility; they must be more competent than their male colleagues but must not look intimidating or threatening; they must be role models for other women who are building their management careers and, at the same time, must masculinize their behavior without losing their feminine characteristics in order to succeed as managers (Kandel 2006; ILO 2016, 2017).

These social and organizational pressures and impositions shape how women leaders "*should be.*" Some key issues in this respect are discussed below.

"I Don't Have to Choose Between Having a Family, Working, and Being Successful"

The CEOs interviewed claim that finding the balance between being a mother and a manager is not easy, given that having a job position with so much visibility and responsibility makes time management difficult. Being both a mother and a manager implies having two full-time jobs that are not mutually exclusive and that may overlap with each other: establishing priorities and managing time strategically is vital.

The interviewees mention that finding a good balance between these jobs is necessary to reduce the stress derived from having various responsibilities and roles in life. Joan Williams (2004) pointed out that many women in the United States face the "*maternal wall*," whether they decide to have children or not.

This phenomenon usually gets triggered when women become pregnant and/or request maternity leaves,[21] and it affects the treatment and the perception of women by colleagues and bosses as well as the decisions that women make when organizing their family lives.

In this sense, the women interviewed state that companies need to implement policies that allow women to better balance the time allocated to work and family. In a louder and more serious and angry tone, the interviewed CEOs claim that women need to defend their positions and the needs that they have in order to fulfill their roles as both managers and mothers, which they know is extremely challenging. It is clear that this situation will not change unless women start fighting and "*stand up*" for themselves.

Several women interviewed claim that some of the challenges faced during their careers include discussing payment and job promotions, making requests for some flexibility or some other type of help, and the opportunity costs concerning working hours. P10 had a more moralizing vision of what it means to be a manager as well as a "*good mother.*" Motherhood often changes priorities, and, consequently, being a manager ceases to define women's identities. When women become mothers, there is a new person who needs their time, company, and complete attention, and, therefore, women must learn to balance work and family responsibilities.

Many managers state that, at this stage, it is essential to be honest with companies and tell them what they need to continue developing

---

[21]Joan Williams refers to research by Jane Halpert, Midge Wilson, and Julia Hickman analyzing top managers' reviews of professional women's performance and the way in which such reviews plummeted after women became pregnant. This relates, in part, to the stereotype of women that gets activated in managers who start seeing women as irrational and emotional decision makers. The same happened in respect to reviews of women who had just returned from their maternity leaves.

their management careers in the light of motherhood. If professional women are considered a valuable resource for the organization, new policies should be established in order to support them, although this is not always the case. As analyzed later on, maternity leaves are still an obstacle present in women's management careers, given that companies do not always implement policies to support the development of managers at this life stage.

Another problem that women face, especially when resuming activities after their maternity leaves, is learning to balance their activities. Certain work meetings often start at 7:00 p.m., that is, at the end of the working day, and neither managers nor companies' policies consider that this organization of time harms both women's and men's family dynamics. Most of the CEOs interviewed claim that this is one of the most challenging aspects that they have to face. Organizations do not consider modifying or taking these situations into consideration since men find it easier to return late to their homes. Women's cases are more complex given that, as the interviewed managers point out, they are usually in charge of making sure that their children carry out home and school tasks, have dinner, and receive a *"goodnight kiss."*

In other words, my work (as manager) is really 24×7 (24 hours a day, 7 days a week). But, to avoid traffic, I leave in a hurry at 6:00 p.m. or 5:50 p.m. to spend time with them (her children) because they normally go to bed at 9:30 p.m. and, otherwise, I can't see them. I have dinner with them.... There may be exceptions sometimes as I told you... or because I have those networking meetings that I explained that women have to attend and that start after 6:00 p.m.... so then I ask my folks to feed my kids. During the week, they have dinner at 8:00 p.m., and it's hard for me because I'm not cool with having someone feed them and then coming home and putting them to bed.... No. I try to be home at 7:00 p.m. (P11, July 2020)

The truth is that I believe new generations' pressure for flexibility will help make life easier for women. But it's not that flexibility measures are being taken to help women. I think that organizations do nothing to make things easier for women, generally speaking. (...) I sometimes feel that, when it comes to talking about women's issues, people think: "Enough, let's not discuss this anymore." I am tired of always talking about this topic. But the truth is that nothing is being done as regards women's issues because there're no more women: we are underrepresented and underpaid, and that has to be said. (P3, April 2020)

Two of the managers interviewed, who are more than 10 years apart in age, were pioneers in implementing remote working modalities for all company members in their organizations. Although remote working modalities are now natural forms of work based on the public regulatory policies deriving from the COVID-19 pandemic, they did not use to be implemented in many organizations before the pandemic, and there were many prejudices about them when weighed against the criterion of team productivity. P10, for example, works in an organization that trains executives in new management trends and is the youngest manager interviewed.

She started working under this modality during her first pregnancy and maternity leave: She was able to work from home, spend time with her baby, deliver results, and work closely together with her team despite not working with them in person. Team development and trust are other aspects that allow managers to better balance work and family responsibilities. P10 was also a pioneer in the implementation of remote working modalities at a time when this type of work was not so common. Today, this working modality is not only regulated in the organizational culture but also very much normalized.

Today, this is the most normal thing. Today you go to the office, and you run into people in the elevator at 3:30 p.m. that tell you: "I want to avoid the traffic and I'm picking up the kids at school now, so I'll continue working from home later." And this was unthinkable before. It was out of place for someone to tell you that they were leaving at 3:30 p.m. to pick up their kids and that they'd connect again when they arrived home.... And what's the problem? Maybe you started to work at 7 a.m., or you skipped your lunch, did everything you had to do, picked up your children, and then you reconnect for a while to finish pending tasks that may have arisen. (P9, May 2020)

Due to the pandemic and the new configurations of home spaces and tasks, the women interviewed, just like most female workers in poorer socioeconomic conditions, point out that they sometimes had to ask for brief recesses during video meetings in order to attend to issues related to their homes or their children, which generated no tensions or problems within their teams. In this sense, they again stress the importance of companies' promotion of programs focused on men—and not only women—becoming more responsible parents as regards their children and household responsibilities.

In the opinion of the women interviewed, telework or remote work represent opportunities to make schedules more flexible and better organize their routines. However, this working modality actually gives rise to more inequality as regards women facing situations of labor vulnerability. The sanitary isolation measures, virtual education policies, and housework overload caused by the pandemic brought about discussions about certain aspects of the telework law in respect to the care of children and older adults living in the same house, mainly as regards the articulation of paid work tasks and care tasks.

However, and by way of example, tax incentives to outsource care tasks were not discussed for the cases of care recipients living in the same home as caregivers. Moreover, no measures were considered so that women stop being solely responsible for these tasks. This situation's impact on women—in terms of stress, workload, and their labor rights—was not discussed either.

Organizational cultures—under the charge of management leaderships—may allow professionals to manage their schedules with some flexibility without judging them as irresponsible or not sufficiently committed to the organization. P1 discusses an issue related to his female colleagues: the importance of professionals not having to lie to companies, teams, or bosses in order to attend parent meetings or other children-related activities.

The disadvantage of working hours flexibility, from the point of view of family and private life, is having to learn how to balance the intensity of work and personal life as well as having the energy to be both a mother and a manager since *the problem is not the time you leave work, but the state in which you arrive home: worn out, exhausted, thinking about a thousand things*" (P1, March 2020).

Furthermore, P2's testimony reveals a situation that many women professionals live as regards their bosses[22] when they become mothers. In her particular case, P2 was subject to the supervision of one same person for half of her management career, and she mentions that it was very difficult to work with her. Her supervisor discouraged the women in her team and told P2 personally that she would not be able to grow in the company since she had decided to start a family. That supervisor did not think that developing a management career was compatible with having children. P2 claims that her supervisor embodied the stereotype of a woman hardly found in companies today: a *"single baby boomer."*

> *I remember that we needed to change medical plans, and they asked her marital status. Her answer was, "I am married to the Company." She couldn't think about that duality. For her, you had to choose between having a family or working and being successful ... and I had chosen both.* (P2, March 2020)

---

[22]Ramos et al. (2003) refer to Loden's work published in 1987 on male and female leadership, organizing it in a comparative manner and then presenting a transformative leadership proposal (Figure 8):

	Masculine Style	Feminine Style
Operational Style	Competitive	Cooperative
Organizational Structure	Hierarchical	Team
Primary Objective	Succeed	Achieve Quality
Problem-Solving Approach	Rational	Intuitive/Rational
Key Characteristics	Strong Control Strategy Nonemotional Analysis	Reduced Control Understanding Collaboration High Performance Levels

Figure 8 Comparison of Male and Female Management Styles

Following the work by Loden (1987), the male leadership style is viewed as competitive and hierarchical and focusing on results and *"doing,"* while female leadership is deemed as more cooperative and focusing on teamwork and *"being."* The organizational values of the masculine style revolve around individualism, competitiveness, conformism, domination, and control, as opposed to the values associated with the feminine style, which promotes collaboration, commitment, equality, diversity and inclusion, and the development of personal relationships.

Even though it has not been studied thoroughly, Joan Williams (2004) states that men who are fathers face the "*paternal wall*," given the assumption that men are highly competent and consistently perform well simply because they are men. This assumption can both benefit and damage men's management careers. Fathers who occasionally attend to family emergencies or children's significant events can be seen as warm and competent leaders. However, men who request paternity leaves may see their professional development adversely affected. Some men are even afraid to request other family benefits to avoid being judged as uninterested in the company and lacking ambition.

Analyzing the interviews of the male CEOs and the balance between their roles as managers and fathers, I noted two antagonistic situations. Both interviewees agree that their wives were in charge of care tasks and household tasks, but one of them claims that he did not face work conflicts when becoming a father since he had enough flexibility to manage his schedule. He currently tries to set an example for his team by not staying late in the office and also grants flexibility to his employees so that they can spend more time with their families.

On the contrary, the other CEO states that he underwent several work conflicts regarding the time available to share with his family, and he remembers having suffered a lot at certain times of his management career. He specifically mentions having to cancel family vacations and doctor appointments as well as missing school events. In retrospect, he regrets all of this now because it is impossible to make up for the lost time and because everything changes as children grow—they have even reproached him for this over the years. In this sense, he currently instructs men not to give up family moments and to be autonomous and responsible when coordinating tasks with the rest of the team so that projects can continue to be carried out when they are not present.

For the women interviewed, being both managers and mothers goes along the same lines: directing and coordinating people. Being a mother implies having to organize the family structure and coordinate household and care tasks. On the other hand, managers direct and supervise people and corporate processes, and they also coordinate companies' strategies. These women claim that motherhood implies a lot of planning regarding their pregnancies, their maternity leaves, and their return to their management careers. However, coordinating people—as mothers and managers—greatly differs from the responsibilities and coordinating tasks undertaken by their male counterparts. Men do not bear responsibilities related to their children's upbringing, as perpetuated by the normative system and reinforced by social structures and behaviors. Therefore, there is a double inequality—socioeconomic and gender inequality—in the normative organization of family care.

Difficulties in Returning to Work

The beginning of family projects and family projects themselves were decisive and critical moments for all the executives interviewed, whether they decided to have children or not, since they directly impact management careers and require planning new work and home-related tasks. Most of the women interviewed, together with their partners, decided when to have children based on the development of their professional careers and the possibility of buying their own house before the birth of their children. These women wanted to achieve particular objectives in their management careers before considering family planning and development.

On the other hand, those who did not have specific goals as regards their management development did talk with their partners about the type of family that they aspired to have. Many point out that they did not make the decision to focus first on their careers and then on having children and also claim not having chosen a particular moment as the "best time" to start a family. Nevertheless, they do mention having discussed and made plans about this with their husbands so as to be prepared for the arrival of children. All of them describe a rationalization process regarding the development of their management careers and the importance of professional and economic objectives when starting to plan to have children.

Motherhood is usually postponed until certain levels of job and economic stability have been reached. Women look for the moment of highest stability in their management careers in order to start a family, considering economic, emotional, relationship, and career stability. As a result, late maternity has become an emerging phenomenon of current times, given that women seek to reconcile their job success with the desire to become mothers.[23]

For instance, one of the CEOs interviewed claims that she and her husband started trying to get pregnant five years after they got married because her goal was to focus on her professional development and accelerate her growth in the company where she worked. In July 1994, she returned to Argentina from the United States after obtaining her MBA at Harvard University, and, a few months later, she got married. Thus, during the next few years, she and her husband had to dedicate considerable time toward traveling.

At this stage, she invested a lot of time in developing her professional career since, as she worked in one of the most important consulting companies in Argentina, she had to travel for work. However, the plan that they had made did not turn out as expected since they experienced difficulties achieving pregnancy once their professional goals were fulfilled, which postponed the dates that they had first outlined. Contrarily, another woman interviewed and her husband did not plan when to start a family. Still, she did contemplate reaching certain levels of education—such as postgraduate education—as well as certain professional goals before thinking about planning a family.

Some women interviewed reported changing their perspectives when they became mothers. P11 was a manager in a Big Four and became a mother before being promoted to her current position. She remembers that, during her pregnancy, she was concerned about not knowing whether to continue her management career or dedicate herself to staying

---

[23]CIPPEC (2017) notes that the postponement of motherhood is a phenomenon that has been growing in Argentina. In 2001, 32 percent of births were attributed to women aged 30 or older, but, in 2016, that figure increased to 38 percent. This is observed especially in women with higher levels of education.

However, neither the postponement of motherhood nor the decrease in the number of children among women with higher education and professional levels affect the growth of women's participation in the labor market. The gap in labor participation between women and men is higher in cases of couples with children. Even before the COVID-19 crisis, 95 percent of the men with children were part of the labor market, while this percentage fell to around 60 percent in the case of women with children and 65 to 70 percent in the case of women with no children.

home and taking care of her child. She points out that many very talented women decide—or almost decide—to abandon their professional careers at this life stage so as to dedicate themselves to caregiving. Companies can then become key actors and implement labor policies that support and help professional women become mothers and continue their management careers. Many times, motherhood hinders the development of professional managers.

> *The truth is that I had many insecurities and fears, and I went through things that had never happened to me at any other time in my life. And it was like a breaking point for me, which I think is the case of many women. And I didn't know very well what to do....* *I did not know very well how to leave him and go back to work.* (P11, July 2020)

On the other hand, P6 remembers that being a mother was not something that she had dreamed of when she was young. Still, she was sure that she wanted to become a mother since her family had always thought that having children was truly meaningful. However, and at the same time, it was clear that she wanted to continue developing her professional career. She discussed this with her husband, and they both looked for a good time to become parents. However, once they had their first daughter, P6 decided that she did not want to wait long to have another baby. Unlike her, who was an only child, she wanted her daughter to have someone to share her life with, to help her expand social circle, to make her company during their vacations. She wanted both children to find support in each other, to experience a feeling of union. Although her husband was not very convinced, he supported her, even though it took longer than she would have liked. It is clear that family values influenced these women's family decisions around a specific family stereotype that perpetuates such vision.

On the other hand, P10 states that, if she had planned her management career, she would have become a mother after reaching a leadership position. In this way, once her children started school and gained more autonomy, she could aspire to obtain a management position implying a higher level of responsibility and corporate dedication—which may be more difficult to reconcile with motherhood.

However, given that she experienced fast professional growth, she had her first child when she was already a manager. She reflects on how opportunities appear in moments different to those planned based on each person's career. When she was promoted to manager, she was not married to her partner. She also became aware that children would arrive at a moment of her career involving great responsibility. Despite not postponing her decision to have children, she faced many uncertainties—not regarding her job continuity but the management position itself—that did not clear up until she was pregnant.

> *What will happen to my work when I take my maternity leave? How will I help the team develop the projects? How will I make sure that my superiors do not feel that my commitment to the organization is compromised because I need to dedicate more energy to my family? How am I going to come back to work after my maternity leave?* (P10, July 2020)

These evidence female managers' concerns during their pregnancies and the way in which these continue to be present until the very end of their maternity leaves. At the same time, it proves that women plan their families together with their partners.

Maternity Leaves: A Pause in Management Careers?

In the more recent years, maternity and paternity leaves have been placed on the public agenda, given that more and more companies are extending leaves,[24] especially paternity leaves, following the transformations in the configuration of family responsibilities. Although she focuses on the situation of women in vulnerable situations, Laura Pautassi (2013) draws

---

[24]In the book *Las fronteras del cuidado: agendas, derechos e infraestructura* written by Laura Pautassi and Claudia Zibecchi (2013), Pautassi analyzes the situation of female salaried workers who receive 90 to 180 days' paid leaves when their children are born, in addition to any extra paid time off for breastfeeding and/or family care. These policies show clear gender bias given the restrictive nature of the leaves offered to fathers, which last two business days. This "*does not allow for men to effectively exercise fathers' care obligations*" (Pautassi and Zibecchi 2013, 106).

attention to this gender bias. In the cases of marriage, adoption, birth, and children's schooling, men receive monetary benefits, unlike women, who are offered time off. Likewise, this bias is reinforced by legislation and public policy because employers are frequently only obliged to provide childcare or offer the sum of money equivalent to such service to their female workers. These biases are also present when analyzing the lack of rules and policies regarding the care of older adults and sick or disabled people.

Most of the CEOs interviewed, based on their personal experiences, helped women continue their management careers and develop their family projects by implementing policies that allow balancing their activities and continuing their professional development. They argue that maternity leaves can be opportunities to analyze one's management career and to change one's role, transition into a new position, and start a new professional career stage. Some of the women interviewed experienced their maternity leaves as opportunities, but they also faced high pressure and extreme situations during this period of their lives.

The pregnancies of the female executives interviewed were diverse as regards the physical difficulties involved and the impact on their careers and their relations with colleagues and/or superiors. A third of the executives interviewed experienced pregnancy complications that caused them to start their maternity leaves early or to request leaves for medical reasons. Four of the women interviewed planned their maternity leaves and asked for extensions in order to be able to spend more time with their children and better organize their household dynamics.

However, they all admit having continued work projects and addressed work-related problems during their leaves. Five of the women interviewed took only 90-day maternity leaves, and two women in that same group confessed that they felt the need to return to work shortly after starting their leaves because they "missed" being at work. Clearly, pressure is masked as the feeling of missing working and wanting to return to the office as fast as possible. On the other hand, three women interviewed requested their maternity leaves to be extended, while two women requested even longer leaves without pay.

Women who experience health problems during their pregnancies face many obstacles and fears regarding their management career development and the need to reorganize their work lives. All the women who chose to rest during their pregnancies due to medical complications continued working, to a certain extent, via remote tools, while also experiencing many fears and concerns regarding their pregnancies. Laptops, smartphones, and messaging services that allow the safe transfer of documentation are tools now readily available to companies. Such tools changed remote work and make it possible to stay connected with the office. At the same time, it is necessary for women to support and trust their teams as well as to feel supported by bosses who do not make them "*feel bad or guilty for not being able to go to the office, thus making them continue to feel productive*" (P2, March 2020).

P3 confesses that the arrival of children was not easy. She has only one daughter due to her health problems and, thus, became completely focused on her baby's evolution and health as well as her own. At the same time, she had planned to continue working and developing her management career after giving birth to her daughter. She requested her maternity leave and combined it with a few vacation days that she had left in order to make the leave longer. She returned to work four months later and got promoted a few months after that: There was no "*penalty*" in her case.

On the other hand, P10 confesses, in a distressed tone, that she experienced a great dilemma during her first pregnancy since she had the possibility of quitting her job. Given that she experienced a high-risk pregnancy and that her baby spent 35 days in the neonatal care unit, she was concerned about her son's health evolution and whether she would be able to return to work in a position of such high responsibility or not. She remembers that another female CEO made her reflect on the importance of her job and her management career in her life. She suggested P10 to return to work and try balancing her family and work life, considering her baby's health condition. Returning to her management career implied deconstructing "*certain archaic structures*" within the organization since there was no protocol established to support women who returned to work after giving birth. She discussed her needs at each stage, such as working fewer days in the office and more days at home, among other policies.

The women interviewed emphasize that the implementation of corporate policies supporting women to return to their jobs and reintegrate into the office after their maternity leaves is crucial for their management careers. Women need policies that allow them to manage their own schedules and better balance corporate responsibilities with family responsibilities.

P10 points out that being able to manage one's schedule helps balance responsibilities. Meetings starting after 6:00 p.m. affect family dynamics: Women can return home at 8:00 p.m., which means that they have to be away from their homes for 12 hours. Starting work later also allows them to spend more time with their families in the morning or the afternoon; work can be continued when their children are sleeping or doing school activities.

> *I decide when I work. Of course, I stay committed to delivering results, to my team, and to the project, but I don't clock in. Having to clock in complicates my family organization and the amount of time available to be with my son. Children have very specific schedules. I feel upset if I arrive home at 8:00 p.m. because he falls asleep at 9:00 p.m.* (P10, July 2020)

On the other hand, some interviewed executives had very healthy pregnancies and felt incredibly energetic and even "*super powerful,*" to such an extent that their partners and doctors had to ask them to "*take it easy.*" When P3 was pregnant, she was working in an important project in Colombia, so she had to travel a lot. Her husband and her obstetrician constantly reminded her that she was pregnant and that she needed to slow down. They monitored P3's care and constantly repeated to her the particularities of the stage that she was going through at each specific time.

> *I told them, "But I'm not sick, I'm pregnant." I continued living my life. I won't say that everything was normal because, well, I was very sleepy and all that stuff, but I had a relatively high position in the organization and I managed many people and a lot of budgets, and I still did not feel any difference in respect to my peers.* (P3, April 2020)

Only two of the women who extended their maternity leaves requested unpaid leaves. During her two pregnancies, P1 was sure that she
wanted to take the obligatory 90-day maternity leave set forth by law as
well as an optional three-month leave and a six-month unpaid leave so as
to spend an entire year with each of her daughters. She even remembers
that, eight months after the beginning of each of her two leaves, she was
offered professional opportunities that implied significant growth in her
management career. As a result, she decided to accept these new positions
and work part-time because she did not want to face the level of demand
and intensity involved in the positions that she had had before her maternity leaves. In this way, she managed to grow professionally in strategic
positions and pave the way to become CEO.

Cases like P3's are exceptions and contradict the phenomenon that
Elizabeth Ehrlich calls "*mommy track*" (Sidle 2011), characterized by
the decrease in professional development opportunities for women who
decide to take time off or work fewer hours in order to focus on their
homes and families. A new stage began when her daughters started primary school at all-day institutions, and P3 could focus more on her career
and take on a position involving greater responsibility and a more intense
workload.

> *I mean, in both cases, I knew perfectly well that, at least until both
> girls started primary school, I didn't want a high-intensity position.
> For me, that was very important because primary school is different,
> because they start going to all-day schools.... It's different. So that was
> a "must" for me.* (P1, March 2020)

P9 was the only manager interviewed who continued working while
on leave. She currently has four children and, in retrospective, would
change some of the things that she did during her maternity leaves. Now
that she has a leadership position, she insists that the women and men
in her team respect their time off and even request extensions to their
leaves. In all her pregnancies, she requested the 90-day maternity leaves
set forth by law, and, when she was pregnant with her last child, and
given the public exposure of her role, she worked from home during the
leave period. Even though this situation was not stressful in her opinion,

she does not recommend it to others so that they avoid overloading their bodies and minds.

> *You freak out thinking about everything that can happen if you're not there, and the truth is that nothing happens. You come back and the role's the same. And if you create solid teams and trust them, when you come back.... You freak out and worry, and the only difference when you come back is that you're more tired at night because your brain's not as trained as it was. When you come back from your leave, you're exhausted at night because your brain's exhausted, because your brain's no longer used to that level of demand.* (P9, May 2020)

All the men interviewed requested the two-day paternity leave set forth by law. One of them combined such leave with vacation days, and, since his work was goal-oriented, he had more flexibility to manage his schedule and be with his partner during her leave. One of the other CEOs interviewed could not manage his schedule in such a way, and, thus, he implemented policies in the company, which he oversees so that both men and women can be together when their child is born.

P14 claimed that fatherhood was a new experience that was guided by his wife and that gave him the opportunity of being a father. All of his children experienced health problems at birth, and, in retrospect, he thinks that he should have taken more days off to be with his family. "*And today I would take many more days than I did.... I don't even remember how many I took, but it must've been around 10 days. It's almost nothing and it's ridiculous*" (P14, May, 2020). As a result of his experiences, he implemented and extended paternity leaves in the company that he manages.

Maternity and paternity leaves are still subject to discussions not only in Argentina but also in other countries of Latin America and in the rest of the world.

In Argentina, the previous administration was working on a bill to modify the current system of leaves that after extensive debate in Congress was approved by the Senate's Labor and Social Welfare Committee. This bill proposed the following changes, among others: leaves for adoption, premature delivery and assisted fertilization; extension of the period of prohibition for mothers to work before and after giving birth (50 days instead of 45); and 10-day leaves for non-birthing parents after the birth of their children.

The current public administration is also working on some changes regarding maternity leave. They have presented a bill to the Congress that is currently under review. The changes include the prohibition on women working 45 days before delivery and 45 days after delivery (being able to reduce pre-partum rest by 10 days and use them postpartum). Women must present a medical note with the estimated date of delivery to the employer, and the preservation of employment and full enjoyment of allowances and rights are guaranteed. With respect to paternity leave, the current administration has not proposed any changes to the current law.

Even though the CEOs interviewed consider that addressing these issues is vital for the continuity of professionals' management careers, public policies and business policies have not yet managed to eliminate inequality and gender stereotypes regarding family responsibilities.

Life Partners

All the CEOs interviewed agree that developing their corporate careers and reaching leadership positions while managing the time available for their families could not have been done on their own. Both male and female CEOs were able to develop their professional careers and manage their time between work and family thanks to their life partners—who share the same goals and support their corporate careers—as well as family and paid care and support networks.

The husbands of seven of the CEOs interviewed have freelance jobs and were able to manage their schedules when their wives started their maternity leaves. These family dynamics—the woman being an executive and her husband being a freelance worker—allow for better managing household routines and organizing family schedules and activities. Having more flexible schedules and working from home helps men be more present in their children's upbringing and during crucial moments of their development. The husbands of two of the CEOs interviewed used to work under employment agreements and could not extend their paternity leaves to be with their wives. However, these female executives claimed that the organization and distribution of housework was shared and that they felt supported even though their husbands had to return to work immediately after the birth of their children.

They define their husbands as *"teammates"* and *"life partners,"* understanding that having children is a shared life project[25] that has to be developed and managed by both of them. Given the current changes in family dynamics, these women claim that *"fathers do not help; fathers breed their children."* The interviewees stress that, when starting a family, both members of the couple must be clear that they will not settle and that they will seek a way to develop professionally without abandoning their management careers.[26]

The interviewees' opinion contradicts the family analysis carried out by Collier et al. (1997) and Durán (2014). These authors consider households—the domestic space—as places that do not allow women to have possession of themselves but, instead, of others, given that women have a double function in families: reproduction and caretaking. On the other hand, being a man and being a father are not exclusive functions

---

[25]In *Un nuevo régimen de justificación: la ciudad por proyecto*, Luc Boltanski (2017) takes the concept of "projective city," often used in the business and management world, to describe changes in family representation. Companies are made up of a variety of projects associated with different people who, in turn, participate in a variety of projects. Likewise, projects have specific objectives and a limited time: They constantly come to an end, become replaced, adjust their priorities and needs, and even modify their schemes and work teams. "By analogy, we can claim that there exists a social structure by projects or a general organization of society by projects" (Boltanski 2017, 188).

[26]Sandberg (2013) claims that one of the most critical decisions in women's professional careers refers to staying single or not as well as choosing the right partner. "I don't know any woman in a leadership role who is not fully supported by her partner. There are no exceptions" (Sandberg 2013, 65). This idea of "making your partner a real partner" goes against all analyses claiming that only single women can reach the highest management positions.

because men are considered social beings who carry out activities that can have effects outside the family dimension.

The women interviewed stress the importance of leaving work problems at the office and not to take them to their families and households. Considering both physical and mental exhaustion, partners' support becomes essential to professional career development. Professional women with management careers in progress need to have very well-organized home structures as well as a life partner who shares their goals, "*rows in the same direction*," and is present at those moments that these women miss because of their jobs.

> *Both men and women can have successful careers if they communicate, if they respect each other, if they know that the other person's career is important and must be taken care of. This implies communicating and balancing things every day because, when there are sudden trips or decisions to be made, maybe one of you has to be put first. I believe that communication is very important, and it is essential to bear in mind that the other person's career matters as much as your own.* (P10, July 2020)

The interviewees argue that it is not healthy for men to take vacation days to be with their families when their partners are on maternity leave. Furthermore, they also argue that men spending more time with their children and helping with caretaking and upbringing is not a solution because it does not ultimately help strike a balance between, in a conventional (and stereotyped) sense, the professional and personal spheres of lives, for men as well as for women. This can especially be the case when the partners work for different companies with different organizational cultures and, thus, different policies about maternity leaves. Nevertheless, many of the executives interviewed claimed that their husbands took small breaks from work or organized their work routines in ways that would allow them to be present during the first months after the birth of their children, such as lunch breaks and early returns from work. This relates to Torrado's (1980) analysis of family units as well as the behaviors and beliefs directly associated with social classes and the material reproduction of such conditions.

Family members must truly take each other into account and be able to differentiate their relationships[27] in order to take care of children and, at the same time, cultivate relationships among them. *"Families would have clear borders (...) Families would have a place where members could be together and take care of their children. (...) Finally, family members would feel affection for each other"* (Collier et al. 1997, 3–4)

One of the executives interviewed states that, after having her second child, she and her husband had the opportunity to better organize their schedules since they already had experience and were conscious about the amount of time and energy that the arrival of a second child would require. Hence, her husband took a two-week vacation to be able to be with her during her second maternity leave. At that time, there were no national laws or a corporate culture allowing men to extend their paternity leaves. The female executives interviewed pointed out that companies look down on men who take many days off to support their wives when they are on maternity leave or to attend to family emergencies. Thus, it is clear that public policies regarding family development are needed so that men can be with their families and take center stage in care tasks. In addition, certain paradigms and cultural habits need to change to support the transformation of women's and men's respective roles in the family.[28]

---

[27]The dynamics of individual members of families revolve around production, reproduction, and consumption, but all of these are always based on their individual experiences, sex, generation, and the social class of its members. The level of commitment and the behavior of members are established according to the place assigned within the family unit in relation to kinship, sex, and age. Thus, the domestic unit itself and its activities are constantly changing. Following this approach, families and everything related to the domestic work are considered as part of the public sphere, which are inherent in the State and the society:

> *Families and the domestic world are shaped in relation to the public world of services; legislation; social control; medical scope; the regulation mechanisms of the prevailing social images regarding families and "normality"; education institutions and ideologies; the social definitions of the location; and the purpose of philanthropy and public charity.* (Jelin 1984, 12)

[28]During a Women's Conference organized by Globant, the CEO of a big consulting firm claimed that, despite the corporate advances as regards women's rights, *"there is a very important challenge as regards women, which is deconstructing this paradigm that women have a period in their lives exclusively dedicated to*

The men mentioned by the interviewed CEOs, as well as their families and commodified networks, took part in children care tasks, actively participating in their upbringing and supporting the family so that women could continue their management careers. In addition, these men often offered emotional support and encouraged their wives' professional development in pursuit of creating a joint life project. Being a life partner implies supporting women's professional development and helping them continue growing professionally. The women interviewed stress that their life partners stood—and still stand—by their side; they did not compete with their careers, and they never considered their own management or professional careers more important than their wives'.

Throughout the interviews, the executives mention some advice for balancing private life and professional life. I will refer to a sort of "*Female Managers' Manual*" including the following tips:

- Learning to be patient with yourself
- Finding your own balance
- Accepting that women are not perfect and that we must stop seeking perfection
- Accepting our mistakes
- Learning how to say **"*no*"** and set boundaries
- Learning how to ask for help
- Having a person to lean on (be it a partner, a friend, a mother, or another relative)
- Accepting that we cannot face all challenges with the same level of commitment
- Learning to take more risks

Learning to ask not only for help, but also for that position that we think we want or deserve—and knowing that a man is always going to be considered first. Also learning to ask for it or to knock on the door and say: "Hey, how is it that the person next to me is doing the

motherhood. That's stupid, and we should keep reflecting on it. Moms are dedicated to motherhood, dads are dedicated to fatherhood, and there are many women and many married and unmarried couples of any gender who are not going to have children. We assume, so to speak, certain cultural thoughts" (Globant 2020d).

same job as me and has the same role and position that I have, but earns more than me?" In other words, we tend to accept whatever comes our way as if it were fine. We need to change our mindset. (P11, July 2020)

P4 mentions the long conversations that she had with her husband about changing her position in a company that was being sold. She aspired to become CEO in another company, breaking through the professional ceiling. Her partner's support made her reflect on her career and the difficulties that women face when visualizing the ideal moment to take crucial leaps in their careers and valuing their potential as professionals. As a result of these conversations, she decided to meet with a headhunter, and she was offered the opportunity to become CEO in an important financial company. After nine months, she applied and was selected for the job.

I was like, "A CEO? Me?" And my husband said, "Obviously." These people are crazy (laughs)… Choosing me to be the CEO of the company. Both my husband and my previous boss told me, "P4, I don't know what is it that you can't understand." (P4, April 2020)

I read the requirements—they were ten so to speak—and I felt that I met seven of them. I didn't meet three of them… And for me, if I didn't meet all ten requirements, then I couldn't apply. And my husband told me: "You meet almost all of them. I mean, what do you care about those three? What you have is more than enough." (P4, April 2020)

At the same time, this *"Female Managers' Manual"* also considers couples. The interviewed executives point out that, in order to develop a functional system that allows for the development of a management career and dedicating time to the family, it is essential to share romantic moments and activities with one's partner. However, many admit that making time for these moments is not always easy. As from the moment you decide to have a partner and plan a common life project, it is crucial to learn to make time for yourself for the benefit of your relationship. The executives stress that, as it happens with family, the quality of time—not spare time—is more important than the quantity of time. The activities mentioned by the interviewed executives include going out to dinner with their partners on a weekly basis, organizing romantic dates (such as anniversary celebrations, walks, and movies), playing sports, sharing hobbies and projects, and organizing trips during the year.

> *For me, investing in your partner is an investment in your children's mental health. I don't feel guilty at all.* (P1, March 2020)

Going Against Nature? Childless Managers

Social changes have given rise to generational gaps among women. As a result, women are now beginning to question traditional gender roles that would only consider them for children's upbringing and other general household tasks. Women have an internal debate regarding their professional development and the pursuit of autonomy and the social importance of being a mother.[29] In addition to this self-debate, they are socially stigmatized if they do not want to have children and accused of being selfish or going against their nature and gender roles. At the same time, in order to reconcile their personal lives, management careers, and motherhood, they develop sequential life projects. Many women, hence, choose to postpone motherhood to their professional careers.

The factors involved in women being older when having their first child include the following: the biological clock (women who wait until they turn 30 or more to have children, which implies the possibility of

---

[29]In her book Madres arrepentidas. Una mirada radical a la maternidad y sus falacias sociales, Orna Donath (2016) analyzes regret and the situations of 23 women who became mothers, analyzing their emotions and rational thoughts after the birth of their children. She conceptualizes their feelings and their conflicts as regards their desire not to become mothers as well the actual fact of being mothers to their children. To conclude, she reflects upon their regret about becoming mothers and also upon issues related to time and decisions as well as society's mistrust in women who say that they regret having become mothers.

not being able to become pregnant or undergoing more complex pregnancies); social stigma (culture, society, and even family's opinions about being a mother); and income (women who decide to have certain financial stability in order to become mothers and/or who decide to have children at a certain point in their management careers so that their possibilities of being promoted are not affected).

Three of the CEOs interviewed did not have children for different reasons. One important factor in these three cases refers to the rationalization of the choice to postpone motherhood, understanding that this decision would imply facing great risks when trying to have a child. This rationalization is not necessarily shared by their partners and sometimes led to conflicts that, in some cases, have not been solved yet. Likewise, postponing motherhood is directly related to the decision to continue working and focusing on the management career as well as job and professional promotions—in these cases, motherhood is associated with obstacles to that job development.

P7 has been in a relationship for five years and has begun to consider different life projects, such as moving in with her partner and starting a family, which are decisions that must be made by both of them. Given her current position, she thinks that her job would not be at risk if she had a baby. She and her boss have been working together for several years, and he has been training her to continue growing at the company. At the same time, she is undergoing a stage in life when priorities are not only related to work and her management career—which, in the past, had required her exclusive and complete dedication—but, instead, to her relationship and her family.

> *I am more focused on forming my own family and really having material time to dedicate myself to my family. I wouldn't like to take on a position requiring a lot of material time and possibly damaging my relationship with my partner or with my future child. Today, I am not interested in this. Tomorrow, maybe I am.* (P7, May 2020)

P7 thinks that she will focus on her professional growth at the organization where she currently works in a more distant future because she currently wants to focus her energy on starting a family. Postponing motherhood and starting to think about it in her 40s are a consequence of several decisions made throughout her professional career. At first, she was focused on her work and professional career. This contributed to her not facing the problems in her relationship, but, at the same time, it protected her from the social mandate—and the family pressure—of having a partner. She remembers that, in her 30s, she was deciding on the type of partner and relationship that she wanted to have. However, at that time, she did not feel the need to start a family since this was incompatible with her management career and continued to focus on her career and job advancement, networking, new experiences, and traveling.

At present, she is more connected with her life project, and, thus, work has been pushed into the background. Although she puts all her energy into work during office hours, she tries to dedicate the rest of the day to herself, her personal matters, her boyfriend, her future family, and to understanding that self-fulfillment is not only linked to job success. In P7's case, late motherhood is the consequence of her search for career and professional development as well as her search for a partner who is on the same page as her and supports her in wanting to be a mother and continue her professional growth.

P5 also started "*to work on her family project*" when she was 38, and she underwent artificial insemination treatments that did not work. Although adoption is another way to start a family, her partner was not entirely convinced of this option. The delay in her maternity project was strictly related to the development of her management career. She had three partners during her life, but she only discussed the possibility of starting a family with the last one.

> *I've never had problems with my personal life. I am not a mother, and all my friends are... because I was always different. For my generation, a 45-year-old woman who was married 3 times, who didn't have a child by the time she was 40, and who had a career...*[30] *Your family starts to look down on you until they realize that, maybe, your motivations are connected to something different.* (P5, April 2020)

---

[30]I observed a sad expression on the interviewee's face.

She began to feel family pressure when younger members of her family were having children in a chronological order that was not followed by her. She remembers that one of her cousins, who is two years younger than her, became pregnant with her third daughter at the age of 40 and found it difficult to tell her the news since P5 had been trying to get pregnant for several years without success. Hence, she stresses that she is aware of the possible consequences of starting to plan a family after the age of 30. She considers that not having been able to have children protects her from social criticism since saying that one does not want to have children gives rise to a lot of social and family criticism. The decision of late motherhood involves dealing with changes in women's anatomy related to fertility eggs decrease as well as facing insemination processes while continuing the development of the management career—she even had to give herself injections in the workplace.

> *I focused on my career although I was part of a generation that would tell you that being a mother and being successful was difficult. When I was 38 years old, my partner, who's one year older than me, and I started looking for a baby, and he'd say, "I can't believe what's happening to us." But why? Because men are fertile during a longer period of time than women. So, I didn't understand how he couldn't get it. I'm 38 years old. Of course this can happen.* (P5, April 2020)[31]

She considers that she was more aware than her partner of the consequences that continuing developing her management career and cultivating her relationship would have on the project of having children. P5 considers that women are more aware of time because women's fertility period is shorter than men's. In P5's case, the decision of late motherhood is a consequence of her search for career and professional development as well as her biological clock and the changes in her body, which, at last, made it impossible for her to get pregnant despite undergoing various medical treatments.

---

[31] I observed angry body language. The interviewee's tone of voice was higher, and her facial expression indicated sadness.

P4, on the other hand, is aware that she postponed her decision to start a family, but she does not consider that this decision was made based on her professional career. Instead, she considers that this was a personal decision and that she was fully aware of its possible consequences. She sought professional help in order to find a supportive environment to reflect on her decisions and the way in which her work and management career impacted her private life. On the other hand, she mentions that starting to think about a having a family implied finding a *"life partner"* sharing her vision and supporting her professional development. In her case, motherhood did not mean having children of her own since her husband has two daughters from a previous marriage that she considers her family today.

I don't have time to be with someone who doesn't want to decide on a project without looking at mine. This doesn't guarantee success either, but it helps clearly establish what we both want. And so, we knew that we both wanted to form a family, although we were in very different places because he'd already had children. (P4, April 2020)[32]

Despite the inner work carried out throughout her life, P4 began to feel social pressure because she was not married and did not have children. She thinks that women are expected to comply with certain gender-specific social conventions, such as being married, having children, and starting a family at a certain age. They generally face disapproving comments within their circles of intimacy and community when they do not follow more traditional life projects.

Argentina is quite open, but when you're asked this in other countries, especially more traditional ones like Colombia or Venezuela or countries in Central America... you are the woman at the table, and they ask you, "Husband?" No, I don't have a husband. No, I don't have children.[33] It was difficult. At some point, you feel the pressure, which is still present. You're the weird one, so to speak. But then, each person's personality will determine how much it affects them. Today, it's still

---

[32]An expression of happiness is observed in the interviewee.
[33]I perceive exasperation and anger in the interviewee's tone and voice.

there, and perhaps what affects me the most is that social views on my personal life determine professional views on my position. Entering a place, men look at you as saying, "And what can you contribute?" When a man walks in, they're not thinking that. (P4, April 2020)[34]

Reconciling family and professional development is a challenge that women continue to face despite changes in societies and organizational cultures. Balancing a personal life, a management career, and motherhood responds to having decided on a certain life project and mainly requires, according to the interviewees, the support of a life partner committed to managers' professional development. However, this book also notes the importance of professional and nonprofessional care networks. Management careers and motherhood are not mutually exclusive life choices but are a set of actions and decisions that people undergo throughout life. At the same time, new generations of women do not feel identified with the mother role and are breaking with socially pre-established gender roles. Whatever the case, however, women continue to face certain social stigmas regarding their gender roles and what is *"expected from them."*[35]

Female Managers' Manual

In addition to the aforementioned challenges, some women claim that the visibility of their current positions and the fact of being public figures in the labor market contribute to evidence the discontent of women in such leadership positions. These situations are relatively common among female executives in very high corporate positions and are related to what is known as the impostor syndrome[36]—women' unconscious fear of not

---

[34]I perceive an angry tone of voice.

[35]The interviewees state that these expectations come from their partners, their immediate families—especially their parents—as well as peer managers and professionals who have both a family and a management career.

[36]William McDowell, Nancy Boyd, and Matthew Bowler (2007) describe that the impostor phenomenon involves the following: feelings of falsehood about one's intellectual capacity; the belief that individual success is based purely on luck rather than hard work or talent; lack of confidence about previous successes; the fear of being evaluated by others and the fear of failure; the fear of being exposed as an impostor; and the incapacity to enjoy personal achievements.

being qualified for the position which they hold or are offered due to the traditional social models and the values instilled in them throughout their lives.

Pauline Rose Clance and Suzanne Ament Imes (1978) began to use the term *impostor syndrome* to name an internal experience that some women in high-performance leadership positions went through. Certain stereotyped social gender dynamics contribute to the development of the impostor syndrome. Women having reached high academic and/or professional achievements believe that they do not have the necessary characteristics for the position given or the goal achieved and consider that such accomplishment derives from having managed to "*deceive*" others. In their research, Clance and Imes noted that this phenomenon is more usual in women than men. Many women feel that they are a fraud and cannot own and recognize their professional achievements. As a result, they feel that they are not worthy of the success and recognition that they have achieved. This syndrome can even translate into self-sabotage and limit the scope of maximum potential[37] of women in management or leadership positions.

Considering the development of the "*Female Managers' Manual,*" the interviewed CEOs stress that it is crucial to be grateful to those who offer help during one's professional development and to be clear about the things that are important and that one wants to do as a professional. One quality that defines managers is the ability to learn from other women and male executives. Female managers should stop asking for permission to occupy more senior positions and begin to acknowledge their professional skills. One of the male managers interviewed claims that managers learn how to lead based on the leadership that they experienced firsthand.

---

[37]One of the male executives interviewed mentions Isela Constantini's confession—Former President of General Motors and Former President of Aerolíneas Argentinas—in Human Camp. She admitted having suffered from hoarseness when she became the head of General Motors Brazil in Brazil and consulting with specialists who could not find any physical problems whatsoever. He remembers talking to her and concluding that it was more of a psychological issue because she was about to formally accept her new position in the automotive industry, which is an industry clearly dominated by men.

For me, the first rule to be a leader is to be who you are and not to copy others. You shouldn't be like an impostor who disguises as someone they are not; you can see through these people right away and you know they can't be good leaders. I believe that the first thing you must do to be a leader is to focus on yourself; to know what you are and what you want; to understand your strengths, the things you like to do, your weak points, your miseries, and the chinks in your armor, because we all have them in my opinion. (P12, May 2020)

In this sense, these female executives stress that being authentic as well as understanding the potential of team members and continuing to learn from them allows professionals to build their leadership. In a conscious or unconscious manner, managers learn from the qualities of others. Analyzing P7's experience, I note that professionals are constantly learning about their roles as managers as well as developing their professional profiles and management qualities. P7 remembers that her team had female and male managers with very strong personalities.

As a result, she found it difficult to exercise her role as director since, on several occasions, she made decisions different from those of her team members. Her own vision as well as that of the team many times collided with the CEO's decisions, giving rise to conflicts and frictions. Being a manager becomes more complicated and lonelier when decisions have to be made and not all team members agree. Still, some situations can teach managers a lot and allow them to position themselves differently and to foster new types of communication within the team. P7 claims that managers must be able to recognize complex situations and to differentiate decisions that must be made by managers from those under the charge of the direction and management team.

According to the interviewees, CEOs must trust the expertise of the directors and managers in their team. They also need to understand how to delegate and manage resources. For such purpose, it is necessary to stay focused on adaptation as well as the organization's achievements and projects; to comprehensively understand the team's skills, the personal experiences that each member is going through, and the way in which these influence their professional careers; and to support different management styles.

Understanding what each person can contribute to the organization, the context necessary for those contributions to happen, the position of each person in the workplace ... Based on that, I have to see how I can manage that person's growth and work to make them successful for the organization, considering each person in a more comprehensive way. (P7, May 2020)

Even though the CEOs interviewed notice many changes as regards what it now means to be a good manager, leader, or CEO, few women currently hold strategic leadership positions because they must still pay the price of not having partners or children and continue to be stigmatized in their executive roles. Some of the interviewees claim that certain female executives continue to disregard other female managers' hard effort, decisions, and conflicts, thus denying gender disparities within teams and companies.

For me, it's unbelievable. I can't believe that there are still women, who I know struggled a lot to get where they are... Because it was difficult for all of us, even for those who say, "No, I've never had problems" and I'm like: "Stop fucking around. Think about your career... You can't tell me nothing's ever happened to you. Think about it for like 3 minutes and I'm sure you will come up with thousands of examples." Women my age... I am 45 years old... We have normalized it. (P5, April 2020)

It is generally assumed that women focused on the development of management and leadership careers neglect their families and the comprehensive development of their children. However, the CEOs and managers who faced these obstacles stress the importance of continuing to work on labor laws and transforming the organizational culture around practices oriented toward work–family reconciliation.

Female Manager Checklist

Balancing the time allocated to the professional career, family life, and personal care involves managing people and available time effectively, establishing priorities, and understanding what aspects and activities can be given up to balance different life projects. In this sense, the executives interviewed agree on the importance of creating traditions or moments to share with their families free of work-related issues, such as childcare tasks, school and social activities, and special events. Women find it difficult to balance their time when resuming their management careers after their maternity leaves and find a way to "*take it easy.*"

They must fight against the uncertainties typical of this stage and allocate time and space to their management careers, their roles as mothers, their self-care spaces, and their relationships. The women interviewed claim facing doubts due to the stress and the difficulties in balancing their different activities. They, however, do not regret continuing their management careers and even mention colleagues who did give up their careers and now, having grown children, regret it.

The healthy thing to do is to find the right balance to fulfill ourselves as professionals, as mothers, as whatever we want and choose to be. And today, I look back and I don't regret my decision to continue my career. (P11, July 2020)

The need to balance time around childcare tasks changes as children grow up and gain greater independence and autonomy to manage certain aspects of their routines: school activities, extracurricular activities, hobbies, sports, and plans with their friends. Many of the women interviewed point out that their children, as they grow up, complain or ask them specific questions about the time that they spend together. As a result, these women explain the demands involved in management careers so that children begin to "*normalize*" working mothers and understand that their professional careers are part of their life choices and are typical of adults.

None of them experienced any conflicts with their children in this respect. They, however, mention that relating with similar families helped their children accept these dynamics when they were young. On the other hand, they argue that it is essential to feel passionate about the management career and firmly believe in what is being done in order to manage times and balance different activities. Flexible work schedules allow women to work at different times, fulfill work projects' objectives, and have time to engage in family activities.

My work helps me connect a lot with who I am. And sometimes it doesn't have to do with what I'm asked to do, but with who I am… If it has to do with helping someone or putting myself in someone else's place… or trying to get a good deal or to make a good deal… I have lots of fun doing that. So, I sometimes use my personal time for that. (P1, March 2020)

In this sense, these women find ways to adapt their work projects to motherhood. P10, for example, used to travel for work once a year and would take her baby, her husband, and their nanny in order to support their family structure and respect their family traditions.

We have paid for flights and hotel rooms for the nanny to pull this off. I've also had to negotiate with my husband so that he would come with me. You also need to negotiate with yourself to make it through motherhood and decide what you can give up and what you can't. During the first two years after having my baby, nights were sacred to me because I was breastfeeding my son. (P10, July 2020)

Most of the women interviewed consider it important to respect family moments, to be fully present, and *"not to be looking at their phones so as to be 100 percent present."* They mention that the quality of time shared with their families is more significant than the amount of time assigned thereto. Moreover, they stress the importance of being present during their children's most critical moments, which often implies re-scheduling their own activities and which may affect the time allocated to their partners. They further claim that finding time to share with their partners is vital. In order to achieve a good work–life balance,[38] self-care

---

[38]All the women interviewed agree that, when there is no time available, women are the adjustment variable as they are the ones who end up missing their activities—such as going to the gym, meeting friends, talking with other adults, and carrying out recreational activities. They, however, agree that this is a temporary situation that changes as children grow up. This issue is typical of women and is evidenced by the survey on the use of time. Care and domestic tasks and/or the administration of resources to carry these out are mostly undertaken by women and impact their lives in different manners—for instance, as regards paid work and/or self-care tasks.

activities shall be paid attention to—either leisure activities, physical exercise, sports, hobbies, or activities with friends. Many executives make time for their activities by multitasking. For example, they read while commuting; they exercise while listening to music; or they spend moments in the morning doing exercise or meditating. One of the managers interviewed summarizes it as follows:

> *As my girls got older—they are already 17 and 20—I resumed leisure activities that were very good for me: I started taking guitar lessons again, I started repertory classes, I started taking singing classes again, I do yoga, I meditate… I take tennis classes on Saturday. I do a lot of activities apart from my work, my daughters, and my family. These are very important moments for me, and I respect them a lot.* (P1, March 2020)

Male CEOs were asked about the implications of being both managers and fathers, although this is a bit more complex issue. Many of them claim that their partners had more responsibility in respect to parenting tasks. However, they all mention family activities or critical moments that they were not willing to give up for their management careers. Weekends are an example of these, and, in order not to miss them, many managers scheduled company trips accordingly. They further state that they do not miss birthdays and, to a lesser extent, school events and medical appointments. Male managers point out that vacations are the time of the year when they share the most with their families.

For the female executives interviewed, being both managers and mothers requires balancing the time available to perform the tasks inherent in each of these roles. Many times, these tasks overlap, and such roles end up complementing each other. Executives must know how to manage their time and routines and what they are not willing to give up and that they should have support networks: These aspects will guide the decisions that they make at each stage.

Moralizing Motherhood

Being a mother as well as the concept of motherhood throughout history are social, cultural, and political constructions of beliefs and meanings that evolve constantly and that are supported by the ideas revolving around women, procreation, and upbringing.[39] Motherhood is a concept constructed by the society, and, therefore, its interpretation and repercussion on individual experiences are crucial and have become one of the most historically significant aspects of women's self-definition. Transformations in the concept of motherhood reflect the influence of cultural processes in social exchanges. These cultural processes evidence that what is considered valid at a particular time depends on the traditions and the temporal and spatial context and will not necessarily continue to be valid in the future. Adding to the complexity of this process, the meanings associated with being a mother and a woman seem to have intertwined. The role of women has ceased to be wholly focused on procreation and child rearing, which have become options that can be relinquished. The identity of mothers and the rituals associated therewith are factors that have adapted to these current times when women are more active in the labor market but continue to be present nonetheless.

The interviewees mention being afraid of not fulfilling their roles as mothers and managers as well as not having enough quality time available to be with their families. Seven of the female CEOs interviewed claim feeling stress, fear, and uncertainty when making certain decisions during their management careers. Having to travel and spend many days away

---

[39]Corina Enríquez Rodríguez (2015) studied the concept of social maternalism as regards Latin American social policies. Mothers are mediators between children and the national government: They receive and manage the money received by government social programs.

These programs are implemented by governments with a double objective: supporting the income of those facing greater difficulties when trying to access a monetary income and, on the other hand, bridging the "poverty trap," that is, the intergenerational transmission of poverty.

These programs have certain requirements, such as children's attendance at school and medical appointments. In this sense, the subjects of right are the children, and the operational beneficiaries are their mothers.

Although the positive impact of these programs on the material condition of women is undeniable, Corina Enríquez Rodríguez argues that they help reinforce the caregiving role of women as well as their role as mothers because only women with children can access these benefits. Finally, she further claims that the national government ends up establishing what "good mothers" must do, assuming that women are the only ones responsible for care tasks.

from their homes and families—often in places with very different time zones—as well as having to live in other locations during short periods for specific projects make them reflect upon the balance between being a mother and a manager. P6, one of the CEOs interviewed, was transferred to a position in the United States while being pregnant and having a young daughter. Despite the stress and the challenges faced on a personal level, she was focused on her work and learned a lot in her new position.

However, from a personal point of view, she remembers this time as a highly complex stage, given her daily routine, the cultural differences as regards professional care networks (in nurseries, babies were treated with little affection and were left to cry), the stress derived from the change in location (which also contributed to her baby not eating and crying a lot), and the difficulties in her relationship (her husband did not have a job and this hindered their family dynamics to such an extent that, due to a domestic accident that compromised their baby's health, they decided return to Argentina and thus prioritize their family over her management career).

Although these women have flexibility to balance times, they faced certain extraordinary situations that made them miss crucial moments in life. For instance, P9 could not be present for the birthday of one of her children due to an urgent trip involving many people from abroad. She does not try to play the victim, but she mentions that it caused her great stress, pain, and guilt.

After the birth of her first child, P10 felt that she was spending little time with her son. Her baby would be asleep both when she left to work and when she came back, so she could only spend an hour of quality time with him, which made her feel upset and anxious and think whether to continue with her management career or not. P3 feels that society still pressures women not to work and to stay home and take care of their children. In this sense, seven of the interviewees claim that, in order to reconcile their roles as mothers and managers, they had to allocate part of their salaries to hiring a professional care network, such as a nanny. At the same time, they find it vital to also have a family support network and, especially, to be supported by their partners in order to be able to pursue their professional development. Some generations still question women who go back to work after having children. P2 points out that she often feels such social pressure, but she chooses to "*ignore*" it. Her firm belief in her professional development and the life project built with her partner help her balance the time available for her family. However, she still worries about whether that available time is enough for her children, but her choice is thorough.

> *I always did what I thought was best, and time will tell. And, in the future, my children will tell me what they think. I always wanted them to see their mother happy, so I think it is a good example for them to see a person who enjoys what she does.* (P2, March 2020)

All the executives consider that managers must know how far they are ready to go and what they are willing to do for the job since certain family issues may have to be given up. In addition to the feelings of guilt and uncertainty associated with raising children, some of the women interviewed also mention feeling guilty as regards their organization and performance in work projects.

> *There were moments when I felt pressure and guilt, and I thought: "I'm going to take the day off. How do I tell my boss? I'm going to take 3 weeks or I'm going to take a long weekend?"* (P8, May 2020)

The interviewees consider that labor policies need to establish more flexible work schedules in terms of presentiality. Remote work modalities have evidenced that the performance, fulfillment, and success of projects are not directly related to the physical presence of people in companies' offices. Due to the new technologies, it is now possible to be connected with one's team from anywhere in the world.

For the women interviewed, "*being a good mother*" does not depend on the amount of time shared with the children but, instead, on the quality of time and the respect for family traditions, which involves communication, active listening, and support in face of children's uncertainties. Many claim that, over the years, they have learned that the quality of the time shared with their children is evidenced by some of their children's physical behavior. Women who are both mothers and managers need to accept that they are going to miss certain family moments. The activities that women share with their children are connected with their households, schools, health status, and families (Figure 9).

		Bath time
Home Rituals		Family dinner
		Putting children to bed
		School functions
School Rituals		School meetings
		Helping children with their homework
Health Rituals		Medical appointments
		Visiting family
Family Rituals		Sports
		Birthdays

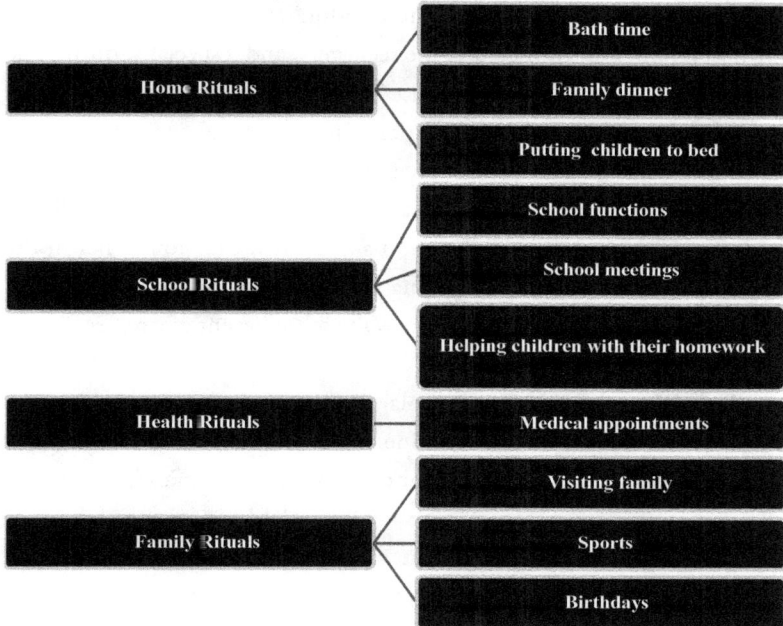

Figure 9 Family Rituals

Source: Own research based on the interviews carried out.

Concerning the rituals related to childcare activities and household routines, four of the women interviewed set a bath time routine to share and play with their children. Six women prioritize family dinners, when they talk about each member's day, listen to their children's concerns and the relevant events in their lives, and give them support. Even though women do not return early from the office during some periods of the year, many families have dinner together and use that moment of the day to have meaningful exchanges. Six of the women interviewed further referred to bedtime, when they sing or tell stories to their children, as a moment that they do not give up for any other activity—either work, relationship, or personal activities.

P1, for example, never compromised putting her daughters to bed and giving them a *"goodnight kiss."* In order to do this, she sometimes scheduled business trips during the day, left very early in the morning, and came back home in the last available flight, which meant starting her day as early as 3:00 a.m. It is essential to follow this routine as from the birth of children until they become teenagers, and, especially, during the breastfeeding time and the first years in children's lives.

Regarding school-related activities, nine of the managers interviewed adjusted their schedules to attend parent meetings and school events. P2 mentions that, during school functions, she loved seeing her children look for her with their little eyes and smile when they found her in the audience. P6 remembers negotiating with her boss the visit from parent company's executives so as not to miss the school event where her daughter was flag bearer.

Both P2 and P6 claim that planning presentations and schedules in general is vital to follow a routine. At the same time, they stress that the role played by family support and care networks—grandparents, uncles and aunts, cousins, and so on—is essential because they help support children and are also present in school functions and events. In this sense, P9 states that family support is critical to children's activities, especially when two of her children were in primary school and two were in kindergarten. Today, her children are in high school and primary school, which helps her better balance her responsibilities and fulfill her different roles.

Only one of the women interviewed mentions helping her children with their homework and learning activities, regardless of the time when she arrived home. Concerning health-related issues, four of the women interviewed claim not missing their children's pediatrician appointments and balancing such appointments with work meetings for considering doctor's visits a priority. Strictly analyzing family rituals, eight of the women interviewed set specific times during the week and the weekends—a kind of "*timesheet*"—to share with their children. These rituals included having a snack or having tea, going for a walk during the weekend, visiting family, attending sport events, and sharing outdoor activities. However, considering all the family rituals, five of the women interviewed stated that birthdays are moments that can never be missed. P1 remembers that, for the birthday of one of her daughters, she took a cake to school at the time when she was supposed to receive an important call from Spain; although it was a stressful moment, she does not regret such decision.

On the other hand, discussing the meaning of being *"a good father"* with men was much more complicated because they do not usually reflect on this. Men are not expected to modify their professional careers when they have children. They were even surprised to realize that this issue— instead of their professional achievements—was the central topic of the conversation. After the initial awkwardness and upon contextualizing the topic hereof and their possible contribution to this work, these men stress, just like the female CEOs, that it is essential to establish routine rituals with their children, such as weekend and school activities. One of the CEOs interviewed claims that he learned that the roles of fathers and managers do not compete with each other but, instead, complement each other. However, he points out that the following is true in some exceptional cases:

People who say, "I left my family for my job" are wrong. Sometimes you have to be at work, and family has to understand. There are times when... Sometimes I tell this to the people that work with me... If your child is sick or you have to go to your child's school function, you can't miss that. No job is worth the complaints that may come later. The secret is to find that balance. These roles do not compete; they are complementary. (P14, May 2020)

However, they mention feeling guilt and remorse—sometimes self-derived and some other times derived from children's complaints— for not having been more present at certain stages of their children's lives. Despite acknowledging having shared crucial and significant moments, they wish they had been more present in their children's day-to-day lives. At the same time, they consider that these reflections are typical of the transformations in mothers' and fathers' roles that have been taking place in recent years and that break with the parenting models that prevailed when they were children.

Children's upbringing entails social gender roles that associate women with reproduction, family, affection, and obedience, and men with power, intelligence, strength, and leadership. These values are translated into practices and games instilled in children: Girls play with dolls, play cooking games, and play teacher and hairdresser, while boys play with balls and cars, and play building games and physical games. (Lewis 1997)

Care Networks and Career Support: "We Have a Small SME at Home"

As stated in Chapter 2, discussions around care economy derive from feminist economists with a different perspective on economy. Following the analysis of Corina Rodríguez Enríquez, the concept of care refers to "*all the activities and practices necessary for the daily survival of people in the society where they live. This includes self-care, direct care of others (interpersonal care), the guarantee of the necessary preconditions for such care (cleaning the house, grocery shopping and meal preparation), and care management (schedule coordination, taking the children to school and other institutions, supervising paid caregivers, among others)*" (Rodríguez Enríquez 2015, 36).

Care involves all the actors participating therein: care recipients (including children and older adults) and caregivers (including family support care networks and professional paid care networks as well as the interrelationships between different actors). Care networks involve social actors, institutional actors, legal and regulatory frameworks, the commodification of care tasks, and community and family relationships, which are fundamental to societies' social capital. Care networks and their dynamics are in constant transformation, following changes in societies and varying according to the socioeconomic status.

Each family has different manners to organize people's care as well as their households. In this sense, all the female managers interviewed have the possibility of accessing paid care services. These services may refer to people who carry out household chores, nannies who care for their children, health personnel trained to care for older adults, or private care institutions such as daycare centers, nurseries, private kindergartens, and private schools (which may be accessed directly or through the company where these women work). One of the executives interviewed compares care activities and household organization to company management:

> *The truth is that we have a small SME at home because, on the one hand, we increased the working hours of the person who helps us with the housework, and, on the other hand, we also hired a babysitter.*

And, as soon as my son turned one, he started going to a daycare center and, when he was two, he started going to kindergarten. Considering the domestic worker, the babysitter, and the kindergarten, we say that we've set up a company to support our family, but I think it's only for a few years. (P10, July 2020)

However, when it is difficult for a single person to carry out certain tasks, domestic workers become incredibly helpful. The professionals interviewed state that, at certain developmental family stages, part of their salaries was allocated to arranging a professional support network in charge of childcare and household organization. Without an organizational structure, it is impossible to balance the responsibilities inherent in professional life and family life.

Likewise, taking into account these interviews, family care networks are crucial for developing childcare support networks and help women continue developing their professional careers. Employing domestic and care staff is a complex and delicate process that must be carried out by the family members responsible for the children and/or older adults. Such family members must together decide who to hire and how to organize their schedules as well as voice their opinions on family organization and development.

The managers interviewed claim that, just like when they applied for their current leadership positions, they carried out comprehensive interview processes, especially in respect to nannies, and made final decisions together with their partners. For the recruitment and selection of childcare workers, they made use of company tools, dynamics, and logics to be able to feel safe and trust the person hired. Family organization involves interrelations similar to those present in corporate environments, and the effective administration of resources allows managers to balance their times and careers.

P3 hired a headhunter to select her daughter's nanny and placed cameras in her house to control their routine and the nanny's work—who was a kindergarten teacher. P3, as many of the interviewees, argues that nannies are trusted with the most important people in the world: their children. Hence, these women consider that it is not excessive to hire a consultant to recruit and interview potential candidates who will deal with their children's affective development, safety, protection, and stimulation. They used optimal business processes for their private life organization. As a result, they were able to spend more quality time with their families and be present at children's critical moments—in the case of families in which men have independent jobs that allow for schedule flexibility and greater presence at home, and, thus, manage care networks and monitor their development.

Three of the women interviewed hired live-in domestic workers when their children were very young. They needed help taking care of their very young children while returning to their full-time management positions. Routines become more complex, and delegating becomes necessary. When P2 had to work on challenging projects demanding more time and energy, she considered it vital to have trained care workers who could take care of bathing her children, making dinner for her family, waking her children up in the morning, getting them ready for school, and taking them to follow up doctor's appointments.

Three executives mention employing live-in domestic workers for a fixed period of time; during the first years after the birth of their children, they considered it necessary to have a person overseeing meal preparation and household organization in general. However, as their children grew up, they were able to come up with different household organization schemes. They are now more comfortable with hiring household workers who perform their tasks on certain days of the week and do not live in the same house as them.

All the CEOs interviewed employ domestic workers who work on certain days of the week. Their tasks include cleaning and tidying the house, washing the clothes, and preparing specific meals. These executives claim that domestic workers become essential in respect to household chores. Therefore, it is necessary to treat them with great respect and attend to their salaries—raises, overtime, vacations, and so on—to avoid job rotation considering the trust placed in these workers who are welcomed into the privacy of their homes. However, all the women interviewed stated that, despite trusting and caring for the women in charge of their household activities, they still consider them as people outside the family, as employees fulfilling specific roles within their homes. One of the women interviewed summarizes her experience as follows:

> *The truth is that I set everything up and I was lucky. I mean, I have a person who takes care of my house, who works very well, and who never takes a day off... I was lucky... lucky to choose her. And you try not to lose that person, so you treat her well and pay her well. In short, you take care of her.* (P9, May 2020)

Five of the women interviewed had—or have—nannies who took care of their children and were almost considered part of their families. In these cases, care falls outside the family and is commodified. Care workers manage children's routines, schedules, school activities, extracurricular activities, eating habits, health problems, playing habits, and so on.

> *If you have two little girls sitting at the table, it's not the same having a woman come in and just feed them than having someone who asks them about school and their activities, who integrates into their lives. It is different. Having an emotional bond changes things. This woman would've given her life for my daughters, and still would.* (P1, March 2020)

> *We couldn't do everything we do now if we didn't have a person who, most importantly, adores my daughter and who knows her schedules and school activities and takes her to different places and then picks her up. We wouldn't be able to do our activities if we did not have someone to support us.* (P3, April 2020)

> *For me, choosing a nanny was a deal breaker to return to work. In other words, I wouldn't have returned to work if I hadn't found a person to trust with the care of my son. I couldn't go to work and leave my son with just anyone. So, we decided to turn to recruiting, and the truth is that it was fantastic, very effective. She spoke the same corporate language, she came from a corporation, and we ended up hiring an exceptional nanny that helped me leave my son without worries. She is still my son's nanny and she's going to be the nanny to my new baby.* (P10, July 2020)

One of the executives interviewed mentions that her daughters considered their nanny a third grandmother who was present—and still is—at important family events, such as birthdays, and continues having a relation with them now that they are teenagers. Considering care workers as family is directly related to the fact that such workers share children's daily lives and routines with them: They eat together, pick them up from school, help them with their homework, fix their clothes, organize their routines, and bond with them.

Although domestic workers organize housework and childcare, parents are still in charge of certain childcare tasks. In previous chapters, I explained the idea of family rituals, that is, family activities within each family. One of the managers interviewed and her husband categorize tasks as *"logistic tasks"* and *"inner world tasks."* Her husband is in charge of logistic tasks, which involve transportation: He is the *"family's Uber."* On the other hand, she takes care of conflicts, school problems, clothing, and changes in look.

On the other hand, one of the CEOs interviewed mentioned that her husband retired from corporate life to work as a freelancer, and, as a result, he is in charge of day-to-day household and childcare tasks. He makes all decisions in respect to household management: paying taxes, deciding on the family meals, grocery shopping, and addressing their children's school or emotional problems. In addition, three of the CEOs interviewed began to delegate some housework responsibilities to their children as they grew up—especially concerning cleaning and tidying up their personal spaces.

> *They are neither ladies nor princesses... It's over. Besides, I realized the girls were not taking the responsibilities they had to assume.* (P1, March 2020)

Families are affective care networks[40] of great significance to female managers since, in many cases, they replace private nurseries. These

---

[40]Feminist theories question the welfare perspective that regards families as main providers of welfare and organization of paid and unpaid work. In this sense, they analyze that inequalities are not only evidenced by the differences in individuals' social and economic development but also evidenced by the domination of a hegemonic masculinity implying divisions between men and woman as regards the symbolic capital.

institutions are seen, by some women, as a last option to take care of their children's development, given their detachment in caregiving.[41] Family's support and proximity help managers better coordinate family routines. One manager's parents, who are very active, live 15 blocks away from her house. Furthermore, this executive also managed to organize her children's routine and activities—school, pediatrician, and sports club— within a 1-km radius of her home.

The male CEOs interviewed acknowledge that care networks and housework division were always managed by their wives, regardless of their employment situation. Just like women, they recognize the importance of having an organized structure of domestic workers, primarily when both partners work outside the home. In addition, they regard family support networks as affective care systems that help balance management careers. Two of the executives interviewed consider domestic workers as part of their families, given the number of years that they have worked in their homes and the close relations that they have with their children.[42] One of the male managers interviewed states that he shares home organizing tasks equally with his wife and that, as their children grow up, they divide tasks further so that children can also collaborate. In his opinion, these tasks are a way of disconnecting from the stress of work. He also claims that this is the way in which he was raised since, during his childhood and youth, he was responsible for certain domestic tasks at his home.

Parent Care

Discussing the administration of elder care networks was more complex because several of the female executives interviewed have active

---

[41]In addition to their male spouses' support, "female executives develop a domestic support network combining family support (from parents or parents-in-law) and, fundamentally, commercialized services (maids, nannies, caregivers, etc.). Matters most linked to affective care are never completely outsourced" (Luci 2016, 142).

[42]The continuity of these employment relationships depends greatly on the affective relationships built between care workers and the children under their charge as well as their employers—especially female employers. Since care tasks imply affection, these employment relations give rise to particular dynamics involving all family members.

independent parents who take care of themselves and are, in fact, part of their children's care network. On the other hand, some women interviewed did not feel comfortable discussing their parents' care. Most of the executives' parents carry out several leisure activities and have wide social circles that provide emotional support and help them with their daily routines. At present, most interviewees perform the following elder care tasks on a routine basis: visiting their parents, providing financial support and help, accompanying them to doctors' appointments, assisting them with administrative issues, and talking with them on the phone.

The interviewees' children call their grandparents and talk about their day and school news, and they also teach them to use new tools such as WhatsApp, Zoom, and Netflix in order for them to stay connected through technology and have new entertainment and recreational possibilities. A particular case is that of P4: When she had to relocate to the United States for work, she installed Skype on her parents' computer and set its automatic execution. At that time, two of her brothers on her mother's side as well as her uncle on his father's side passed away, so she was constantly worried about receiving a call about something happening to her parents; she was living far away and could not have done anything in a quick manner.

Most of the female CEOs interviewed organized, together with their siblings, a system to assist the older adults in their families in case of emergency. Their tasks depend on their proximity, their working hours, and their responsibilities toward their own children—in case they have any—and their financial situation. One executive's mother is sick, and, thus, that executive, together with her siblings, is supporting her during this moment of her life.

The good thing is that I'm not an only child facing this situation. All of us, even my husband, help, and we adapt to support her at this moment. I'd never taken such a leading role as regards my parents' care. At some point in life, this situation touches all of us closely.... I've been lucky. Both my parents are here, and they're 80 years old. I'm very lucky. I'm going through all of this quite late in life. Some people experience it much sooner and they have to take charge when they're still very young. (P2, March 2020)

Given the COVID-19 health crisis, some of the managers interviewed had to change their routines in order to assist their parents. They helped them with their grocery shopping, provided financial and emotional support, and taught them to use their computers to access bank and online shopping websites, Netflix, and Zoom. At that time, one executive's parents were living in another province. Therefore, she decided to move them into her home in order to support them during the quarantine and be closer in the event of any health inconvenience. Another manager built a house on her parents' land and, at the time of the quarantine, moved there with her family to be with her parents during that period.

As regards the men interviewed, one of them claims that his father lives an independent life and works, and they talk on a daily basis. Another CEO mentions that his sister lives on the same land as his mother, and, therefore, she is the one in charge of care tasks that may need immediate attention. However, they both have a smooth communication flow with the professional staff caring for their mother in order to coordinate their schedules. This CEO started a ritual with his mother: Every time he travels to Brazil for work—two or three times a month—he visits her on his way to the airport. Furthermore, he applies a company management model to her mother's care organization. She is an active woman, and, hence, the activities that she carries out need to be balanced with the tasks performed by the professional care staff. In this way, she can be taken care of without giving up what she likes doing.

Many female managers undergo their transitions to *Chief Executive Mom Officers* when they decide to start a family and have children while continuing to develop their management careers. Professional women's decision about whether to have children or not is influenced by cultural and family factors. Additionally, planning becomes a key factor if they intend to continue developing their management careers. Despite the benefits of women being included in the formal employment system as professionals, women still face inequality as regards the development of their careers and the obstacles encountered. As stated in the interviews, a way to address these issues may lie in the joint work between companies and the national government so that new public policies help women to continue their professional development and men to get involved in childcare tasks.

CHAPTER 4

What's Next?

Women in leadership positions face a number of challenges related to gender inequality, gender stereotypes, and conflicting demands on their time and energy. Balancing the demands of their careers with their roles as caregivers can be particularly difficult, as women often feel pressure to be available and present for their families while also being dedicated and effective leaders in their workplaces.

As regards family, the most significant difficulty faced by women refers to balancing their roles as mothers and their roles as managers in terms of the amount and the quality of time dedicated to their children and family development. All women face the *"maternity wall"* regardless of whether they decide to have children or not. However, this mainly affects women who decide to start a family: Their decisions are viewed differently, and they are attributed with emotionality and irrationality, which affects their dynamics with colleagues and bosses.

Women who decide not to have children or postpone motherhood to reconcile it with their management careers face a cultural battle against the stigma of being selfish or going against their gender's nature. They feel pressure from their inner circles (their families) and from others (colleagues, bosses, friends, etc.).

These women constantly worry about being unable to fulfill their roles as mothers and managers, perform efficiently at work, and be present at crucial moments in their children's lives. They suffer a double guilt burden because they fear not being able to meet the company's objectives or their role as mothers, based on them having to miss certain life moments so as to balance their times, objectives, and tasks.

One strategy that may be helpful for women in this position is to seek out support and resources that can help them manage their time and responsibilities more effectively. This might include delegating certain tasks or responsibilities to family members or hired help, as well as being more intentional about how they structure their time and prioritize their commitments.

Another important approach is to challenge gender stereotypes and biases that may be limiting women's career opportunities and advancement. This can involve advocating for oneself and seeking out opportunities to take on leadership roles, as well as actively working to create a more inclusive and supportive workplace culture that values and promotes diversity and gender equality.

Women face a "*glass ceiling*" due to the discrimination suffered and the lack of corporate policies supporting their professional development. As a result, women's management growth is hindered, and, in some cases, women stop seeking job promotions or pursuing their professional development, which gives rise to the idea that they cannot be part of decision-making processes.

However, women's professional development is not only affected by these external factors. There are also internal factors, known as the "*concrete ceiling*," which hinder women's professional development to such an extent that highly qualified women decide to reject job promotions but continue to take on more responsibilities and/or modify their schedules in order to reconcile work with motherhood.

Such internal barriers and the feeling of not being qualified or deserving of a promotion, together with the lack of confidence and the fear of failure, are known as "*imposter syndrome*," which is mainly experienced by women. This phenomenon arises within specific stereotyped social gender dynamics that cause women who have reached high academic and/or professional achievements to believe that they do not have the necessary qualities for the position given or the goal achieved and to consider that such accomplishment derives from having managed to "*deceive*" others.

It is important for companies to actively work to address these issues by implementing policies and practices that support gender equality and diversity in the workplace. This might include measures such as offering flexible working arrangements, providing mentoring and training programs, and promoting a culture of inclusion and respect.

This is evidenced by the need of female managers to be supported by their bosses, mentors, and sponsors in order to climb the career ladder and integrate into leadership and networking spaces. These spaces, however, do not only have socialization purposes; they are also used for making business outside of normal office hours. However, since they have been historically built and inhabited by men, they are incompatible with family life.

The empirical evidence shows that the masculine management career model adversely affects both women and men because they need to adapt their behaviors and actions to such model. There is, however, inequality in this regard. On the one hand, men feel more comfortable reproducing this model because women usually assume the responsibility of sustaining families as well as care structures. On the other hand, and as the interviewees describe, women often face gender discrimination.

Most companies have guides that include definitions of managers, their desired skills, and the ways to achieve the goals set, thus giving rise to companies' successful leader archetypes. On the other hand, this work has evidenced the existence of an informal and unexplicit guide as regards "*Chief Executive Mom Officers.*" In this "*Female Managers' Manual,*" the rationalization of private life, family organization, and children care are considered from the perspective of management careers' business logics and values.

Such "*Female Managers' Manual*" includes attitudinal issues related to patience and the search for balance in life by managing the time allocated to families, partners and management careers. For this purpose, learning to ask for help and lean on trusted people becomes a key factor. Women need to understand that they are not perfect; they must stop constantly seeking perfection in order to prove that they are suitable for leadership positions and accept their mistakes and bad business decisions. The aforementioned manual also refers to the importance of learning to say "no," to set boundaries as regards both professional and family life, to become more audacious, and to trust one's instincts. Furthermore, it is vital to delegate and rely on the expertise and skills of others—team or family members and friends—to complement each other's roles and tasks. Constant work and learning are required to let go of the guilt derived from not being present at all family moments.

Lastly, "*Chief Executive Mom Officers*" stress the importance of quality time over quantity of time, being fully present at family moments without thinking about work, and multitasking in order to manage to carry out self-care activities, work-related tasks, as well as enjoyable activities.

Management logics regarding the administration of material and human resources are present in the development of commodified and non-commodified care networks: Women strategically manage available resources using their own capital in the domestic field. Professional care networks become fundamental as regards family dynamics and, hence, require special attention. Hiring care workers involve considering candidates' professionalism and experience in terms of comprehensive care and education.

Likewise, care workers are expected to develop affective bonds with children and become "*one more member in the family*" (even though they do not share a blood bond), but it is still necessary to separate issues related to the family's personal lives from those related to care tasks. Nannies are trusted to attend to children's affection, education, and safety. They are expected to sit at the table with the children and share meals with them, talk about school, know their schedules, help them do their homework and get dressed, be present in the family routine, and develop affective relationships.

Inequality is an analytical dimension affecting women from the lowest social quintiles as well as female managers at the top of organizational pyramids, which is a group little studied in Argentina. This book provided empirical evidence for a topic of interest on the public agenda. It is worth continuing to study female managers' development and the actions that they take to access the highest corporate levels and negotiation tables as well as the ways in which they balance such roles with family life while simultaneously dealing with inequalities present in all social quintiles.

Bibliography

Adler, Nancy. 1995. "Expatriate Women Managers." In *Expatriate Management: New Ideas for International Business*, edited by J. Selmer. Quorum Books.

Aguinaga, Margarita, Miriam Lang, Dunia Mokrani, Alejandra, and Santillana. 2012. *Pensar desde el feminismo: críticas y alternativas al desarrollo en Más allá del desarrollo.* El Conejo.

Bergara, Ander, Riviere Josetxu, and Bacete Rixtar. 2008. *Los hombres, la igualdad y las nuevas masculinidades.* EMAKUNDE—Instituto Vasco de la Mujer.

Bielby, William T., and Denise D. Bielby. 1992. "I Will Follow Him: Family Ties, Gender-Role Beliefs, and Reluctance to Relocate for a Better Job." *American Journal of Sociology* 97 (5): 1241–1267. http://www.jstor.org/stable/2781415.

Bourdieu, Pierre. 2003. *La dominación masculina.* Anagrama.

Brosio, Magalí. 2016. "Introducción a la medición de la brecha salarial por género y sus determinantes." octubre 18. https://ecofeminita.com/introduccion-a-la-medicion-de-la-brecha-salarial-por-genero-y-sus-determinantes/?v=5435c69ed3bc.

Boltanski, Luc. 2017. "Un nuevo régimen de justificación: la ciudad por proyecto." *Revista de la Carrera de Sociología* 7 (7): 179–209.

Carrasco, Cristina. 2001. "La sostenibilidad de la vida humana: ¿un asunto de mujeres?" *Mientras Tanto* 82: 43–70.

Castro, Carolina. 2020. *Rompimos el cristal.* Paidós SAICF.

CEPAL (Comisión Económica para América Latina y el Caribe). 2005. *Políticas hacia las familias, protección e inclusión social.* Edited by Irma Arriagada. CEPAL.

Cheung, Fanny, and Diane Halpern. 2010. "Women at the Top: Powerful Leaders Define Success as Work + Family in a Culture of Gender." *The American Psychologist* 65: 182–193.

CIPPEC (Centro de Implementación de Políticas Públicas para la Equidad y el Crecimiento). 2017. "Las mujeres tienen cada vez menos hijos y más tarde." Accessed junio 2021. https://www.cippec.org/textual/las-mujeres-tienen-cada-vez-menos-hijos-y-mas-tarde/.

Clance, Pauline Rose, and Suzanne Ament Imes. 1978. "The Impostor Phenomenon in High Achieving Women: Dynamics and Therapeutic Intervention." *Psychotherpy: Theory, Research and Practice* 15 (3): 241–247.

Collier, Jane, Michelle Z. Rosaldo, Sylvia, and Yanagisako. 1997. *¿Existe una familia? Nuevas perspectivas en antropología?* Edited by Lancaster and Di Leonardo (compiladores). Routledge.

Collin, Francoise. 1994. "Espacio doméstico, espacio público en Ciudad y Mujer." Presented at the Seminario Permanente "Ciudad y Mujer," Madrid.

Defillippi, Robert J., and Michael B. Arthur. 1994. "The Boundaryless Career: A Competency-Based Perspective." *Journal of Organizational Behavior* 15 (4): 307–324. https://www.jstor.org/stable/2488429.

Donath, Orna. 2016. Madres arrepentidas. Una mirada radical a la maternidad y sus falacias sociales. Penguin Random House.

Durán Heras, María Ángeles. 1995. "Familia, economía y estado." *Cuenta y Razón* 91: 44–48. http://hdl.handle.net/10261/99944.

———. 2000. "La nueva división del trabajo en el cuidado de la salud." *Política y Sociedad* 35: 9–30. http://hdl.handle.net/10261/100388.

———. 2012. *El trabajo no remunerado en la economía global.* Fundación BBVA.

———. 2014. "La rebelión de las familias." In *La responsabilidad ética de la sociedad civil: Mediterráneo Económico.* Colección de Estudios Socioeconómicos, edited by Adela Cortina. Caja Rural de Almería y Málaga. http://hdl.handle.net/10261/108743.

———. 2016. "El futuro del cuidado: El envejecimiento de la población y sus consecuencias." *Revista de pensamiento contemporáneo* 50: 114–127.

Durán Herrera, Juan José. 2006. *El auge de la empresa multinacional española.* Boletín Económico de ICE.

Eagly, A. H., L. Gartzia, and L. L. Carli. 2014. "Female Advantage: Revisited." In *The Oxford Handbook of Gender in Organizations*, edited by R. Simpson, R. J. Burke, and S. Kumra. Oxford University Press.

ELA (Equipo Latinoamericano de Justicia y Género). 2012. *De eso no se habla: el cuidado en la agenda pública—Estudio de opinión sobre la organización del cuidado.* Edited by Natalia Gherardi, Laura Pautassi, and Carla Zibecchi. ELA.

———. 2021. *Sexo y Poder, ¿Quién manda en la Argentina?* ELA.

Esquivel, Valeria. 2011. *Atando Cabos, deshaciendo nudos—La economía del cuidado en América Latina: Poniendo a los cuidados en el centro de la agenda— Programa de las Naciones Unidas para el Desarrollo.* Procesos Gráficos.

Florencia, Luci. 2016. *La era de los managers: Hacer carrera en las grandes empresas del país.* Paidós.

Gersick, Connie J. G., and Kathy Kram. 2002. "High-Achieving Women at Midlife: An Exploratory Study." *Journal of Management Inquiry* 11 (2): 104–127.

Glikin, Leonardo. 2015. *Iguales y Diferentes: Los espacios de la mujer en la empresa de familia.* Aretea Ediciones.

Globant. 2020a. "Ciclo de charlas con profesionales—Café con Protagonistas: Gabriela Terminielli—'Diseño de carrera y agilidad emocional.' " YouTube, junio 12. https://youtu.be/bs-SBqzDaWk.

———. 2020b. 'Ciclo de charlas con profesionales—Café con Protagonistas: Jorgelina Albano—'Meritocracia y Género.'" YouTube, junio 24. https:// youtu.be/LJ9Y7fLL0sY.

———. 2020c. "Ciclo de charlas con profesionales—Café con Protagonistas: Patricia Bindi—'Liderazgo con propósito.'" YouTube, julio 28. https:// youtu.be/WLgOVt8AWzc.

———. 2020d. "Ciclo de charlas con profesionales—Café con Protagonistas: Tamara Vinitzky—'Emprendimiento y diseño de carrera en organizaciones.'" YouTube, junio 17. https://youtu.be/yle2MaI_lzY.

———. 2020e. "Ciclo de charlas con profesionales—Café con Protagonistas: Cecilia Giordano—'Cuando las mujeres prosperan, los negocios prosperan.'" YouTube, agosto 05. https://youtu.be/c-ghR4cuY8M.

———. 2020f. "Ciclo de charlas con profesionales—Café con Protagonistas: Alejandro Mascó—'Diversidad: El desafío a aceptar y respetar.'" YouTube, agosto 12. http://youtu.be/7VpfMO24YWU.

———. 2020g. "Ciclo de charlas con profesionales—Café con Protagonistas: Virginia Meneghello—'Masculinidades, Género e Inclusión.'" YouTube, agosto 19. https://youtu.be/uXusIj7S8Jc.

———. 2020h. "Ciclo de charlas con profesionales—Café con Protagonistas: Andrea Grobocopatel—'Liderazgo responsable y diversidad.'" YouTube, septiembre 01. https://youtu.be/ofKu6cDsnOI.

———. 2020i. "Ciclo de charlas con profesionales—Café con Protagonistas: Laura Barnator—'Perspectiva de carrera: derribando mitos.'" YouTube, septiembre 14. https://youtu.be/bha3WlvBxOM.

———. 2020j. "Ciclo de charlas con profesionales—Café con Protagonistas: Carolina Castro—'Ser industrial no tiene género.'" YouTube, octubre 16. https://youtu.be/nTsUJiaxEtE.

Hatum, Andrés. 2020. "Tipos de jefes horribles y cómo lidiar con ellos." *IProfesional*, febrero 21. https://www.iprofesional.com/management/309775 -tipos-de-jefes-horribles-y-como-lidiar-con-ellos.

Hewlett, Sylvia Ann, and Buck Luce Carolyn. 2005. "Off—Ramps and On—Ramp: Keeping Talented Women on the Road to Success." *Harvard Business Review.* https://hbr.org/2005/03/off-ramps-and-on-ramps-keeping -talented-women-on-the-road-to-success#.

Himmelweit, Susan. 2005. "El descubrimiento del trabajo no pagado: las consecuencias sociales de la expansión del trabajo." In *Debate sobre el trabajo doméstico: Antología.* Desarrollo Gráfico Editorial S.A. de C.V.

Hirata, Helena, and Daniéle Kergoat. 1997. *La división sexual del trabajo: Permanencia y cambio.* Asociación Trabajo y Sociedad, Centro de Estudios de la Mujer (Chile), Piette Conicet (Argentina).

IDEA (Instituto para el Desarrollo Empresarial de la Argentina). 2018. *Estudio social y empresarial: ¿Qué significa ser iguales? Iniciativa de la Red de Diversidad e Integración de IDEA*. Estiudios Sociales y Empresariales, IDEA. https://www.idea.org.ar/mundo-idea/relevamientos/estudios-sociales-y-empresariales/.

ILO (International Labour Organization). 2016a. *Las mujeres en el trabajo: Tendencias de 2016*. OIT.

———. 2016b. *Young and Female: A Double Strike? Gender Analysis of School-to-Work Transition Surveys in 32 Developing Countries*. Edited by Sara Elder and Sriani Kring. OIT.

———. 2017a. *La Mujer en la Gestión Empresarial: Cobrando Impulso en América Latina y el Caribe*. OIT.

———. 2017b. *Panorama Laboral 2017: América Latina y el Caribe*. OIT.

IMF Business School. 2019. "Soft Skills vs Hard Skills ¿cuál es la diferencia?" Accessed abril 2020. https://blogs.imf-formacion.com/blog/recursos-humanos/formacion/soft-skills-vs-hard-skills-cual-es-la-diferencia/.

INDEC (Instituto Nacional de Estadística y Censos de la República Argentina). 2013. *Encuesta sobre Trabajo no Remunerado y Uso del Tiempo*. Ministerio de Economía y Finanzas Públicas de la Nación.

INDEC (Instituto Nacional de Estadística y Censos de la República Argentina). 2021. *Dosier estadístico en conmemoración del 110° Día Internacional de la Mujer*. Ministerio de Economía de la Nación.

Jelin, Elizabeth. 1984. *Familia y unidad doméstica: mundo público y vida privada*. CEDES. http://repositorio.cedes.org/handle/123456789/3500.

Jelin, Elizabeth, and Gustavo Paz. 1991. *Familia / género en América Latina: cuestiones históricas y contemporáneas*. CEDES. https://repositorio.cedes.org/handle/123456789/3371.

Jorrat, Jorge Raúl. 2008. "Percepciones populares de clase." Paper presented at the Encuentro Latinoamericano de Metodologia de las Ciencias Sociales, UNLP—FaHCE.

Kandel, Ester. 2006. *División sexual del trabajo ayer y hoy: Una aproximación al tema*. Dunken.

Koṭlawī, Abū Yusuf Muḥammad Sharīf Muḥaddiš. n.d. *Akhlāq-uṣ-Ṣāliḥīn*. Maktaba-tul-Madīnah.

Lamas, Marta. 2021. *El dilema de la paridad en Feminismos, cuidados e institucionalidad: Homenaje a Nieves Rico*. Edited by Laura Pautassi and Flavia Marco Navarro (coordinadoras). Fundación Medifé.

Lazear, Edward, Kathryn Shaw, and Christopher Stanton. 2015. "The Value of Bosses." *Journal of Labor Economics* 33: 4.

Loden, Marilyn. *Feminine Leadership, or How to Succeed in Business Without Being One of the Boys*. London: Times Books, 1987.

Lewis, Jane. 1997. "Género, política familiar y trabajo remunerado y no remunerado." *DUODA Revista d'Estudis Feministes* 13: 25–51.

Luci, Florencia. 2009. "Aprender a liderar: los MBA y el reclutamiento de las
Escuelas de Negocios de Buenos Aires—Notas etnográficas sobre el mundo
del management." *Revista de Antropología Social* 18: 317–337.

———. 2011a. "La carrera directiva en el marco de la reconfiguración empresarial argentina: ¿Una 'revolución managerial'?" *Revista Latino–americana de
Estudos do Trabalho* 16 (26): 145–181.

———. 2011b. "Managers de grandes empresas: ¿trabajadores o patrones?"
Apuntes de investigación del CECYP XV (20): 195–203.

———. 2016. *La era de los managers: Hacer carrera en las grandes empresas del
país.* Paidós.

———. 2017a. "El trabajo de mando: los managers de empresas como
objeto de estudio de las ciencias sociales." *Revista Ciencias Sociales* 2017:
114–119.

———. 2017b. "¿Manejadas por sus propios dueños? Las grandes empresas y el
trabajo de formación de managers." *Revista del Centro de Estudios de Sociología
del Trabajo* 9: 31–59.

Luci, Florencia, and Diego Szlechter. 2014. "La sociología del management en
Argentina: debates para un campo en formación." *Revista Latino—Americana
de Estudos do Trabalho* 19 (32): 113–156.

McCraw, Thomas K. 1990. "Reviewed Work: The Modern Corporation and Private Property by Adolf A. Berle, Jr., Gardiner C. Means." *Reviews in American
History* 18 (4): 578–596. https://doi.org/10.2307/2703058.

McDowell, William C., Nancy G. Bowler, and Wm. Matthew Boyd. 2007.
"Overreward and the Impostor Phenomenon." *Journal of Managerial Issues*
19 (1): 95–110. https://www.jstor.org/stable/40601195.

Mercer. 2018. "Two Minutes to Understand Global Mobility Management—A
Compilation of Short Articles Covering: Cost Cutting, Flexibility, Segmentation, Expatriate Gig Workers, Diversity." octubre.

Mills, Wright. 1956. *The Power Elite.* Oxford University Press.

Ministerio de Desarrollo Productivo [Ministry of Productive Development].
2017. "Mapa Cuántas empresas hay en el país, cuánto produce y a qué
categorías pertenecen." Accessed agosto 2019. https://gpsempresas.produccion
.gob.ar/datos-y-ana isis/.

Montesinos, Rafael. 2004. "La nueva paternidad: expresión de la transformación
masculina." *Polis: Investigación y Análisis Sociopolítico y Psicosocial* 2 (4):
197–220. https://www.redalyc.org/articulo.oa?id=72620409.

OCDE (Organización para la Cooperación y el Desarrollo Económicos). 2012.
*Gender Equality in Education, Employment and Entrepreneurship: Final Report
to the MCM 2012.* OCDE.

Oddone, María Julieta. 2014. "El desafío de la diversidad en el envejecimiento en América Latina." *Revista Voces en el Fénix* 36: 82–89. https://flacso.org.ar /wp-content/uploads/2014/08/Julieta-Oddone-voces-en-el-fenix-.pdf.

OIT (Oficina Internacional del Trabajo)—en colaboración con la Unión Europea y Organización de las Naciones Unidas Mujeres. 2019. *La mujer en la gestión empresarial: Cobrando impulso en Argentina—Programa GANAR GANAR.* OIT.

Palomar, Cristina. 2018. "*Madres arrepentidas: Una mirada radical a la maternidad y sus falacias sociales*—Orna Donath, Barcelona: Penguin Random House, 2016." *Debate Feminista* 56: 110–114. https://doi.org/10.22201/cieg.2594066xe.2018.56.06.

Pautassi, Laura. 2013. "El trabajo de cuidar y el derecho al cuidado, ¿Círculos concéntricos de la política social?" *Revista Cátedra Paralela* 10: 65–92.

Pautassi, Laura, and Carla Zibecchi. 2013. *Las fronteras del cuidado: agendas, derechos e infraestructura.* Biblos.

Pautassi, Laura, and Maria Nieves Rico. 2011. "Licencias para el cuidado infantil. Derecho de hijos, padres y madres." In Desafíos, Boletín de la infancia y adolescencia sobre el avance de Objetivos de Desarrollo del Milenio. Santiago de Chile, CEPAL-UNICEF, No 12.

Peterson, Jordan, and Warren Farrell. 2018. "The Absolute Necessity of Fathers." *Toronto*, may 7. https://www.youtube.com/watch?v=v5O_FLUWYmg.

Rama, Betina. 2015. *Liderazgo femenino: Aprendizajes de carrera de ejecutivas latinas.* Libro digital EPUB. https://archive.org/details/isbn_9789873385520 /page/4/mode/2up.

Ramos, Amparo, Ester Barberá, and Sarrió Maite. 2003. "Mujeres directivas, espacio de poder y relaciones de género." *en Anuario de Psicología* 35 (2): 267–278.

Rice, James Mahmud, Robert E. Godin, and Antti Parpo. 2006. "The Temporal Welfare State: A Crossnational Comparison." *Journal of Public Policy* 26 (3): 195–228.

Rodríguez Enríquez, Corina. 2015. "Economía feminista y economía del cuidado: Aportes conceptuales para el estudio de la desigualdad." *Revista Nueva Sociedad* 256: 30–44.

Rodríguez Enríquez, Corina, and Gabriela Marzonetto. 2015. "Organización social del cuidado y desigualdad: el déficit de políticas públicas de cuidado en Argentina." *Revista Perspectivas de Políticas Públicas* 4 (8): 105–134.

Rodríguez Enríquez, Corina, and Laura Pautassi. 2014. *La organización social del cuidado de niños y niñas: Elementos para la construcción de una agenda de cuidados en Argentina.* ELA, CIEPP and ADC.

Rodríguez Gustá, Ana Laura. 2019. *Marchas y contramarchas en las políticas locales de género: Dinámicas territoriales y ciudadanía de las mujeres en América Latina.* Edited by Ana Laura Rodríguez Gustá. CLACSO.

Sandberg, Sheryl. 2013. *Lean in: Women, Work and the Will to Lead.* Alfred A. Knopf, a Division of Random House.

Schmukler, Beatriz Elba. 2013. "Democratización familiar como enfoque de prevención de violencia de género: experiencias en México." *Revista Latinoamericana de Estudios de Familia* 5: 199–221.

Secretaria de Trabajo de la Nación. 2018. *Mujeres en el mercado de trabajo argentino.* Equipo de Mercado de Trabajo. Dirección General de Estudios Macroeconómicos y Estadísticas Laborales.

Sidle, Stuart D. 2011. "Career Track or Mommy Track: How Do Women Decide?" *Academy of Management Perspectives* 25 (2): 77–79. http://www.jstor.org/stable/23045067.

Slaughter, Anne Marie. 2012. "Why Women Still Can't Have It All." *Atlantic,* July/August. https://www.theatlantic.com/magazine/archive/2012/07/why-women-still-cant-have-it-all/309020/.

Tomazic, Ana Cárdenas, Ana María, and Yévenes Ramírez. 2018. *Mujer (es), familia (s) y Trabajo (s) Un debate internacional.* Teseo.

Torrado, Susana. 1980. *Sobre los conceptos de "estrategias familiares de vida" y "proceso de reproducción de la fuerza de trabajo": notas teórico—metodológicas.* Centro de Estudios Urbanos y Regionales.

Williams, Joan C. 2004. "Hitting the Maternal Wall." *Academe* 90 (6): 16–20. https://www.jstor.org/stable/40252700.

Zangaro, Marcela. 2011. "Subjetividad y trabajo: el management como dispositivo de gobierno." *Trabajo y Sociedad* XV (16): 99–100.

About the Author

Rocio Ariela Izquierdo is an accomplished multilingual political scientist from Buenos Aires, Argentina. She graduated from the University of Buenos Aires with a Bachelor of Political Science and moved on to complete a Master's in Management, Development, and Policy from Georgetown University and the National University of San Martin. Her master's thesis is a study on the unique challenges and strategies the female business leaders in some of the worlds most important companies face as they balance their career advancement and family life.

Since very young she developed a keen interest in politics and languages. As a native Spanish speaker, she was driven to study English, French, Portuguese, and Chinese, while participating in several political activities. Her dedication and hard work granted her a Fulbright Scholarship to continue her Political Sciences studies at the University of Texas at Austin. While at Georgetown she wrote several papers on policymaking like "Analysis of the Law of Entrepreneurs of Argentina" and "Comparative Analysis of Maternity and Paternity Leave Between Argentina and Sweden." Both were a prelude to what would later become her master's thesis.

She worked for several NGOs, the most notorious: The American Chamber of Commerce in Argentina and The Institute for Business Development in Argentina. Where she managed some of the largest and most relevant events that mixed the public agenda and the private sectors like the IDEA Annual Colloquium which gathers the nation's President with CEOs of the most relevant companies with operations in the country. She then moved to Vancouver, Canada where she continued her studies while working as an Experience Learning Coordinator at the Sauder School of Business at the University of British Columbia.

Rocio is looking forward to continuing her research in a PhD. She enjoys traveling, gardening, and helping NGOs that work with animals.

Index

Affective care networks, 96–97
Archaic structures, 64
Argentine Institute of Statistics and
        Census (INDEC), 6, 9
Assertive leadership, 52

Bad bosses, 34
Bosses, 31–35, 37, 102

Care
    care of others, 2–3, 92
    defined, 1, 3, 92
    importance of, 3
    measuring, 3
    multidimensionality of, 3
    networks. *See* Care networks
    for older people, 3
    psychological, 3
    responsibility and co-responsibility
        in, 10
    self-care, 3, 13, 83, 84, 92, 103
    unequal distribution of
        responsibilities, 2
    unpaid care, 3n1, 8, 13
    work schedule, 4–10
Care networks, 92
    children, 98
    commodified, 104
    domestic, 15–16
    elder, 97–98
    family, 93, 96–97
    managing, 94
    non-commodified, 104
    nonprofessional, 79
    professional, 79, 87, 104
    unpaid, 3n1
Chief Executive Officer (CEO), 10n5,
        11n6, 35
Children's care network, 98
Communication, 28, 81, 88, 99

Company management model, 99
Comprehensive care, 10, 104
Concrete ceiling, 10–11, 12, 102
Concrete ceiling, 102
COVID-19, 5, 55, 60n23, 99

Discretionary time, 13
Discrimination, 10, 39, 44
    female manager's experience
        regarding, 38
    gender, 37, 45–47, 49, 103
    glass ceiling due to, 102
    pay, 20n10, 45
Division of labor, 6
    gendered, 2
    sexual, 1–2
Domestic work, 4, 6, 8–9, 14, 71n27,
        93–94, 96–97

Economic Commission for Latin
        America and the Caribbean
        (ECLAC), 5
Elder care networks, 97–98
Emotional agility, 44
Empathetic leadership, 47
Employment, 7, 25, 68–69
    activity, 6n3
    formal system, 99
    relationships, 97n42
Equal opportunities, 5, 10
Equality/inequality, 5, 39, 49, 56–57,
        68, 104
    double, 10, 40, 59
    economic, 8, 14
    gender, 2, 4, 8, 10, 43, 59, 99,
        101–102
    pay, 47
    social, 14
    socioeconomic, 10, 59
    workplace, 45

Equity
    gender, 5
    labor, 5

Families, women in, 17–21
Family dynamics, 21n11, 54, 65,
        68–69, 87, 104
Female hysteria, 40
Female leadership, 15, 57
Female managers
    checklist, 82–85
    manual, 79–82
Feminist theories, 96n40
Flexibility, 53–54, 58, 67
    to balance times, 87
    to reconcile professional tasks, 11
    schedule, 94
    working hours, 56

Gender bias, 62n24, 63, 102
Gender-exclusive dichotomies, 1
Gender gap
    in gender gap, 8
    in labor markets, 5
Gender stereotypes, 4, 8, 37,
        40n19, 68
    challenging, 102
    construction, 21, 21n11
    defined, 19n9
    formation, 14
Gendered division of labor, 2
Glass ceiling, 10–11, 26, 102
Good bosses, 32
Good father, 91

Harassment, 37–38, 49–50
Health-related issues, 90
Horizontal segregation, 39, 46

Imposter syndrome, 79–80,
        79n36, 102
Inner world tasks, 96
International Labor Organization
        (ILO), 5, 39, 47

Labor force, 5, 8, 20n10
Labor markets, 10, 45, 47, 51
    changes in, 42
    gender gap in, 5

hierarchical structure of, 20n10
women's participation in, 2, 4–5,
        7–8, 20n10, 51, 60
Leadership, 4, 11n6, 22, 29, 43, 91,
        102–103
    assertive, 52
    building, 81
    careers, 12, 82
    empathetic, 47
    female, 15, 57
    male, 15, 57
    management, 56
    positions, 32–36, 39, 44, 47,
        51–52, 61, 66–68, 79–80, 93
    reasonable, 52
    responsibilities, 13
    roles and responsibilities, 50
    strategic, 82
    styles, 23n12, 24, 31, 41
    transformative, 57
Life partners, 68–74, 78–79
Logistic tasks, 96

Machiavelli, 33
Male leadership, 15, 57
Management careers, 37
    stages of, 17
Management development, rise of,
        23–37
Managerial path, steps into, 21–23
Master Black Belt, 29–30, 29n14
Maternity
    labor regulation on, 10
    late, 59–60
    leave. See Maternity leave
    as obstacle to management
        careers, 46
Maternity leave, 53, 71
    difficulties in taking, 47–49
    first pregnancy and, 55
    in management careers, 54,
        62–68, 83
    maternity wall, 53, 101
    paid leaves for fathers to
        complement, 10n4
    policies about, 70
Maximum potential, 80
Mentors, 31–32, 36–37, 102
Mommy track, 66

Motherhood, 46–47, 58–61, 78–79, 101–102
    changing priorities, 53–54
    due to social or biological factors, 19
    late, 76–77
    mandate, 51
    moralizing, 85–86
    postponement of, 60n23, 74–76

Networking, 32, 36–37, 43–44, 47, 102

Optimal business processes, 94
Organization for Economic Co-operation and Development (OECD), 4–5
Organizational cultures, 21, 24, 56, 70, 79
    inclusive, 22
    transforming, 14, 82

Paid work, 4–10, 13, 15, 56, 96n40
Parent care, 97–99
Paternity leaves, 10, 47, 49, 58, 62, 67–69, 71
Poverty, 5, 86n39
Power elites, 10n5
Pregnancy, 20, 47–48, 53, 55, 60, 62, 66, 77
    complications, 63
    health problems during, 63–64
    healthy, 65
    high-risk, 64
Prejudices, 27n13, 40, 55
Professional development, 23, 26, 28
Projective city, 69n25
Public administration, 68

Rationalization, 59, 75, 103
Reasonable leadership, 52
Remote working, 55
Returning to work, difficulties in, 59–62

School-related activities, 90
Self-care, 3, 13, 83, 84, 92, 103
Senate's Labor, 67
Sexism, 37, 38, 39n18
Sexual division of labor, 1–2
Single baby boomer, 57
Six Sigma methodology, 29n14
Social capital, 36, 92
Social classes, 3, 6, 18n8, 70–71
Social conventions, 78
Social criticism, 77
Social gender dynamics, 80, 102
Social maternalism, 86n39
Social stigma, 75, 79
Social Welfare Committee, 67
Sponsors, 31, 36–37, 102
Stereotypes, 20, 41, 43
    classic, 4
    family, 61
    female hysteria, 40
    gender. See Gender stereotypes
    male, 37
    social gender dynamics, 80, 102
    women, 4, 53n21, 57
Strategic leadership, 82

Time macho, 15
Transformative leadership, 57
Trial and error process, 34

Unemployment, 6n3, 7
Unpaid care, 3n1, 8, 13
Unpaid work, 2, 8, 96n40
    domestic work, 6–8, 14, 71n27, 93–97

Vertical segregation, 39, 46

Women's Conference, 71n28
Working modality, 55, 56

www.ingramcontent.com/pod-product-compliance
Lightning Source LLC
Chambersburg PA
CBHW061332220326
41599CB00026B/5154